Effects of climate variation on the breeding
ecology of Arctic shorebirds

Effects of climate variation on the breeding ecology of Arctic shorebirds

Hans Meltofte, Theunis Piersma, Hugh Boyd, Brian McCaffery, Barbara Ganter, Viktor V. Golovnyuk, Katherine Graham, Cheri L. Gratto-Trevor, R.I.G. Morrison, Erica Nol, Hans-Ulrich Rösner, Douglas Schamel†, Hans Schekkerman, Mikhail Y. Soloviev, Pavel S. Tomkovich, Diane M. Tracy, Ingrid Tulp and Liv Wennerberg

† Doug Schamel deceased 30 March 2005

Meltofte, H., Piersma, T., Boyd, H., McCaffery, B., Ganter, B., Golovnyuk, V.V., Graham, K., Gratto-Trevor, C.L., Morrison, R.I.G., Nol, E., Rösner, H.-U., Schamel, D., Schekkerman, H., Soloviev, M.Y., Tomkovich, P.S., Tracy, D.M., Tulp, I. and Wennerberg, L. 2007. Effects of climate variation on the breeding ecology of Arctic shorebirds. – Meddelelser om Grønland Bioscience 59. Copenhagen, Danish Polar Center 2007. 48 pp.

© 2007 by the authors and the Danish Polar Center

Cover front: Incubating red knot after a snowfall at Cape Sterlegova, Taimyr, Siberia, 27 June 1991. Photo: Jan van de Kam

No part of this publication may be reproduced in any form without the written permission of the copyright owners.
Publishing editor Kirsten Caning
Printed by Special-Trykkeriet Viborg a-s

Scientific Editor:
Erik W. Born, Senior scientist, Greenland Institute of Natural Resources.
P.O. Box 570, DK-3900 Nuuk, Greenland.
Tel. +45 32833800, fax + 45 32833801, e-mail: ewb@ghsdk.dk

About the monographic series Meddelelser om Grønland Bioscience
Meddelelser om Grønland, which is Danish for Monographs on Greenland, has published scientific results from all fields of research in Greenland since 1879. Bioscience invites papers that contribute significantly to studies of flora and fauna in Greenland and of ecological problems pertaining to all Greenland environments. Papers primarily concerned with other areas in the Arctic or Atlantic region may be accepted, if the work actually covers Greenland or is of direct importance to continued research in Greenland. Papers dealing with environmental problems and other borderline studies may be referred to any of the series Geoscience, Bioscience or Man & Society according to emphasis and editorial policy.
For more information and a list of publications, please visit the web site of the Danish Polar Center http://www.dpc.dk. All correspondence concerning this book or the series Meddelelser om Grønland (including orders) should be sent to:

Danish Polar Center
Strandgade 102
DK-1401 Copenhagen
Denmark
tel +45 3288 0100
fax +45 3288 0101
email dpc@fi.dk

Accepted June 2007
ISSN 0106-1054
ISBN 978-87-90369-06-4

Contents

Abstract **7**

Introduction **9**

Study sites and data **13**

The breeding season of Arctic shorebirds 14
    Arrival on breeding grounds 14
    Pre-nesting period and egg-laying 15
    Clutch size and egg volume 18
    Energetic constraints and nest abandonment during incubation 19
    Predation on eggs 20
    Chick-rearing 22
    Total juvenile production and recruitment to the breeding population 25
    The post-breeding period of adults on the breeding grounds 27
    Adult survival and site tenacity on the breeding grounds 28
    Population densities, distribution and size 29

Discussion **32**

Acknowledgements **37**

References **38**

Appendix **48**

Abstract

Meltofte, H., Piersma, T., Boyd, H., McCaffery, B., Ganter, B., Golovnyuk, V.V., Graham, K., Gratto-Trevor, C.L., Morrison, R.I.G., Nol, E., Rösner, H.-U., Schamel, D., Schekkerman, H., Soloviev, M.Y., Tomkovich, P.S., Tracy, D.M., Tulp, I. and Wennerberg, L. 2007. Effects of climate variation on the breeding ecology of Arctic shorebirds. – Meddelelser om Grønland Bioscience 59, Copenhagen, Danish Polar Center, 48 pp.

About 50 species of shorebirds breed in the Arctic, where they constitute the most characteristic component of the tundra avifauna. Here, we review the impact of weather and climate on the breeding cycle of shorebirds based on extensive studies conducted across the Arctic. Conditions for breeding shorebirds are highly variable among species, sites and regions, both within and between continents. Weather effects on breeding are most moderate in the Low Arctic of northern Europe and most extreme in the Siberian High Arctic. The decision of whether or not to breed upon arrival on the breeding grounds, the timing of egg-laying and the chick-growth period are most affected by annual variation in weather. In large parts of the Arctic, clutch initiation dates are highly correlated with snowmelt dates and in regions and years where extensive snowmelt occurs before or soon after the arrival of shorebirds, the decision to breed and clutch initiation dates appear to be a function of food availability for laying females. Once incubation is initiated, adult shorebirds appear fairly resilient to variations in temperature with nest abandonment primarily occurring in case of severe weather with new snow covering the ground. Feeding conditions for chicks, a factor highly influenced by weather, affects juvenile production in most regions. Predation has a very strong impact on breeding productivity throughout the Arctic and subarctic, with lemming *Dicrostonyx* spp. and *Lemmus* spp. fluctuations strongly influencing predation rates, particularly in the Siberian Arctic. The fate of Arctic shorebirds under projected future climate scenarios is uncertain, but High Arctic species and populations appear particularly at risk. Climatic amelioration may benefit Arctic shorebirds in the short term by increasing both survival and productivity, whereas in the long term habitat changes both on the breeding grounds and in the temperate and tropical non-breeding areas may put them under considerable pressure and may bring some of them near to extinction. Their relatively low genetic diversity, which is thought to be a consequence of survival through past climatically-driven population bottlenecks, may also put them more at risk to anthropogenic-induced climate variation than other avian taxa.

Key words: shorebirds, waders, Charadrii, Arctic birds, breeding, body stores, feeding conditions, food limitations, chick growth, predation, severe weather, climate impact, climate change, population bottleneck, genetic diversity, extinction

Hans Meltofte, National Environmental Research Institute, Department of Arctic Environment, P.O. Box 358, DK-4000 Roskilde, Denmark; mel@dmu.dk

Theunis Piersma, Animal Ecology Group, Centre for Ecological and Evolutionary Studies, University of Groningen, P.O. Box 14, 9750 AA Haren, The Netherlands, and Department of Marine Ecology and Evolution, Royal Netherlands Institute for Sea Research (NIOZ), P.O. Box 59, NL-1790 AB Den Burg, Texel, The Netherlands; theunis@nioz.nl

Hugh Boyd, National Wildlife Research Centre, Environment Canada, Carleton University, Ottawa, Ontario, Canada K1A 0H3; hugh.boyd@ec.gc.ca

Brian McCaffery, U.S. Fish and Wildlife Service, Yukon Delta National Wildlife Refuge, P.O. Box 346, Bethel, Alaska, U.S.A.; brian_mccaffery@fws.gov

Barbara Ganter, Schückingstrasse 14, D-25813 Husum, Germany; barbara.ganter@t-online.de

Viktor V. Golovnyuk, State Biosphere Reserve "Taimyrsky", Obrucheva 11-2-33, Moscow, 119421, Russia; golovnyuk@yandex.ru

Katherine Graham, 310 Glasgow Place, Thunder Bay ON P7A 7Y3, Canada

Cheri L. Gratto-Trevor, Prairie and Northern Wildlife Research Centre, Canadian Wildlife Service, Environment Canada, 115 Perimeter Road, Saskatoon, SK S7N 0X4 Canada; cheri.gratto-trevor@ec.gc.ca

R.I.G. Morrison, National Wildlife Research Centre, Environment Canada, Carleton University, 1125 Colonel By Drive (Raven Road), Ottawa, Ontario, Canada K1A 0H3; Guy.Morrison@ec.gc.ca

Erica Nol, Biology Department, Trent University, Peterborough, Canada ON K9J 7B8; enol@trentu.ca

Hans-Ulrich Rösner, WWF Wadden Sea Office, Hafenstrasse 3, D-25813 Husum, Germany; roesner@wwf.de

Douglas Schamel, Department of Biology & Wildlife, P.O. Box 756100, University of Alaska Fairbanks, Fairbanks, Alaska 99775, U.S.A.

Hans Schekkerman, Dutch Centre for Avian Migration & Demography (NIOO-KNAW), P.O. Box 40, 6666 ZG Heteren, The Netherlands; h.schekkerman@nioo.knaw.nl

Mikhail Y. Soloviev, Department of Vertebrate Zoology, Biological Faculty, Moscow Lomonosov State University, Moscow, 119992, Russia; soloviev@soil.msu.ru

Pavel S. Tomkovich, Zoological Museum, Moscow Lomonosov State University, Bolshaya Nikitskaya Street 6, Moscow 125009, Russia; pst@zmmu.msu.ru

Diane M. Tracy, 3865 Potter Road, Fairbanks, Alaska 99709, U.S.A.; dmtracy@hotmail.com

Ingrid Tulp, Institute for Marine Resources and Ecosystem Studies (IMARES), P.O. Box 68, NL-1970 AB IJmuiden, The Netherlands; ingrid.tulp@wur.nl

Liv Wennerberg, Natural History Museum, University of Oslo, P.O. Box 1172, Blindern, N-0318 Oslo, Norway; Liv.Wennerberg@nhm.uio.no

Introduction

Shorebirds, or waders (Sub-order: Charadrii), constitute the dominant component of avian fauna in the Arctic, both in numbers of species and in population densities (Järvinen and Väisänen 1978, Boyd and Madsen 1997, Lindström and Agrell 1999). In contrast to most biodiversity patterns, which show strong clines of lower biodiversity with increasing latitude (e.g. MacArthur 1972, Hillebrand 2004), a number of shorebird genera have most, or even all, species breeding in the Arctic. A total of about 35 shorebird species have their main distribution within Arctic tundra habitat, and a further c. 15 extend their distribution from more southerly breeding grounds into the Arctic (Piersma and Wiersma 1996, Piersma et al. 1996). An estimated 30 million shorebirds breed in the Arctic, out of a global total of 100 million (CHASM 2004). Outside the breeding season, Arctic shorebirds disperse over virtually all temperate and tropical regions of the globe (Fig. 1).

Shorebirds have some of the largest eggs relative to their body size among birds, and most Arctic species are constrained by time to one clutch per season. Thus, high energetic requirements must be met within a short period in an environment where energy expenditure is already high (Piersma et al. 1996, 2003). In the High Arctic, weather is more extreme, the season shorter and the habitat less productive than at lower latitudes (Jonasson et al. 2000), all of which add to the energy demands faced by Arctic-breeding shorebirds. Two additional features of their

FIG. 1. About 50 species of shorebirds breed in the Arctic, but they spend 9-11 months of the year in temperate and tropical non-breeding areas. Before going north in spring, they build up large fat and other body stores on spring staging areas to enable the long flight and to survive the first days on the tundra. Black-bellied plovers, red knots and dunlins at Griend in the Dutch Wadden Sea in May. Photo: Jan van de Kam.

INTRODUCTION

biology may be relevant in the context of rapid climate change. (1) There is co-variation between breeding latitude and non-breeding habitat, with more northerly-breeding species relying to a greater extent on coastal and saline habitats during the non-breeding season than those breeding farther south (Piersma 1997, 2003); such habitats will be especially liable to climate-induced changes in sea level. (2) Most Arctic-breeding shorebird species are genetically less diverse than other birds (Baker and Strauch 1988, Baker 1992, Baker et al. 1994, Wennerberg et al. 1999, Avise 2000, Wennerberg 2001a, Wennerberg 2001b, Wennerberg et al. 2002). This loss of genetic variation may reflect (repeated) population bottlenecks, perhaps caused by earlier climatic changes and extremes, selective sweeps perhaps caused by stringent selection events such as disease episodes, or a combination of these (Baker et al. 1994, Kraaijeveld and Nieboer 2000, Wennerberg 2001a).

Most species of Arctic-breeding shorebirds are

FIG. 2. Map of the Circumarctic with Low and High Arctic zones and study sites marked (slightly modified from CAVM Team 2003 using Bliss 1997 for definitions of the Arctic zones). Large dots with site names denote intensive study sites of the authors as specified in the Appendix on page 48, while small dots denote sites with one or a few seasons of study. Note that the subarctic zone is generally not considered part of the Arctic in this paper, but constitutes the forest-tundra zone south of the Low Arctic. Results from a few tundra study areas in the northernmost parts of the subarctic, however, are also referred to (see Appendix for characteristics of the individual study sites).

confined to certain tundra types and geographical regions, and most breed either in the relatively lush sub- and Low Arctic tundra or on the drier and less productive High Arctic tundra. This means that each species is highly dependent on the distribution and extent of that particular type of tundra, and hence depends on the climatic conditions that shape and maintain the habitat (see CAVM Team 2003, for diversity of Arctic tundra types). Anticipated climate changes are expected to become particularly pronounced in the Arctic, and extensive and dramatic changes in habitat types, snow, and weather regimes are predicted for most tundra areas (Callaghan *et al.* 2005). Although Arctic shorebirds are adapted to the highly variable annual conditions on the breeding grounds, the expected future climate and habitat changes may put them under significantly increased pressure.

During recent decades, large population declines seem to have taken place in both Nearctic and Palearctic shorebird populations (Morrison 2001, Morrison et al. 2001, Morrison et al. 2006, Bart et al. 2007, see however Meltofte et al. 2006a). Based on present knowledge of population trends (known for 52% of the 100 biogeographical populations of 37 species recognized as typically Arctic), 12% are increasing, 42% are stable, and 44% are decreasing, while 2% are possibly extinct. The reasons for these more or less well documented declines are not known, but habitat changes and other anthropogenic disturbance in temperate and tropical non-breeding areas are suspected to contribute (International Wader Study Group 2004).

In this paper we provide a more comprehensive and diverse picture of the response of Arctic shorebirds to weather and climate on the breeding grounds than has been previously available (Boyd and Madsen 1997, Gratto-Trevor 1997, Weber *et al.* 1998, Lindström and Agrell 1999, Rehfish and Crick 2003, Piersma and Lindström 2004). We have worked with shorebirds in virtually all parts of the Arctic for many years (Fig. 2) and have included published, as well as unpublished material, for this review. By compiling existing knowledge on weather and climate impacts on each segment of the annual breeding cycle, and by examining differences between parts of the Arctic, we aim to identify the most critical periods during breeding and thereby facilitate evaluations of potential future impacts (see overview in Table 1). Evidently, Arctic shorebirds are also exposed to climate variability and change during their non-breeding seasons outside the Arctic, but this is only briefly touched upon in this paper (see e.g. Wiersma and Piersma 1994).

INTRODUCTION

Breeding sequence	Problematic weather types	Weather effect	Breeding parameter affected	Consequence of effect	Sub- and Low Arctic western North America	Sub- and Low Arctic eastern North America	High Arctic Canada and Greenland	Low Arctic North Europe	Sub- and Low Arctic Siberia	High Arctic Siberia
Arrival on breeding grounds	cold, storms	inclement weather en route	late arrival, so late nesting	decreased adult survival; decreased or no re-nesting potential; decreased chick or juvenile survival	moderate	moderate to strong	moderate	weak	strong	strong
Pre-breeding period and egg-laying	cold, storms	decreased food availability	late or no nesting	decreased nesting or re-nesting potential; decreased adult survival; decreased chick or juvenile survival	moderate	strong	strong	weak	moderate	strong
	snow cover	small patches of snow-free habitat	late or no nesting; easily searched nest habitat	decreased nesting or re-nesting potential; increased nest predation; decreased chick or juvenile survival	weak	moderate	strong	weak	moderate	strong
Incubation	snow, wind, cold	increased energy use, decreased food availability	more time spent feeding; increased energy expenditure	nest desertion; decreased adult survival	weak	weak	moderate	weak	weak	moderate
	low winter snow cover and temperatures	possibly decreased rodent abundance	increased nest predation; more late nests	decreased productivity	moderate	moderate	moderate	weak	moderate	strong
Chick rearing	cold, wind, rain, snow	decreased food availability; less time to forage (more brooding); increased chick energy expenditure	slow chick growth; chick mortality	decreased chick survival	weak	moderate	moderate	weak	moderate	strong
Post-breeding of adults	cold, wind, snow	decreased food availability	late migration, or decreased reserves during migration	increased adult mortality	weak	weak	weak	weak	weak	weak
Population densities and distribution	cold and late spring	decreased invertebrate productivity	decreased food availability	fewer birds attempting to breed; re-distribution of opportunistic species	moderate	strong	weak	weak*	moderate	strong

*) moderate or strong in opportunistic species

TABLE 1. Matrix deducting the main impacts of weather and climate phenomena during the major sequences of the breeding cycle in Arctic shorebirds together with an evaluation of the strength of these effects during present day conditions in different regions of the circumpolar Arctic.

Study sites and data

We have worked intensively in 13 study areas and less intensively in a number of other tundra sites (Fig. 2). Four study sites are found in sub- and Low Arctic Alaska and Canada, three occur in High Arctic Canada and Greenland, one is found in Low Arctic northernmost Europe, three are found in sub- and Low Arctic Siberia, and two in High Arctic Siberia. (See Appendix for geographical co-ordinates, shorebird species studied, names of contributing authors, study years, and references to papers with site characteristics and work performed.)

For unpublished results, all quantitative statements in this paper are based on statistically significant findings ($p \leq 0.05$) from correlation analyses, linear regressions, paired sample t-tests, chi-square tests and non-parametric Mann-Whitney U tests.

The breeding season of Arctic shorebirds

Arrival on breeding grounds

In some sub- and Low Arctic areas, shorebirds arrive from late April, early or mid May, but in most Arctic areas the bulk of migrants arrive from late May until early to mid June (Meltofte 1985, Morrison 1992, Syroechkovski and Lappo 1994, Nol *et al.* 1997, B. McCaffery, unpubl.). In some sub- and Low Arctic parts of western North America, extensive snow cover has already vanished during May, whereas in the High Arctic and in large parts of the Siberian and eastern Canadian sub- and Low Arctic, snow cover may persist well into June (Mayfield 1978, Groisman *et al.* 1994, Dye 2002, http://climate.rutgers.edu/snowcover). This means that Siberian shorebirds and those in the central Canadian Arctic (north of 65°N) are the latest to arrive on the breeding grounds, sometimes with the bulk of birds arriving as late as mid or even late June (Syroechkovski and Lappo 1994, Tomkovich *et al.* 1994, Paulson 1995, Smith 2003, Tulp and Schekkerman 2001, Tomkovich and Soloviev 2006). In most Arctic areas shorebirds arrive directly on the tundra, because coasts are ice-covered well into the breeding season, but they may spend some days in favorable communal feeding areas before they disperse on territories.

Most Arctic shorebirds fly into the Arctic from distant final spring staging areas in temperate regions – sometimes over distances of more than 4000 km (Alerstam 1990, van de Kam *et al.* 2004, Piersma *et al.* 2005). Because weather in these areas is poorly correlated with conditions on the breeding grounds, the timing of migration of Arctic shorebirds appears to be dictated by long-term average conditions in the respective parts of the Arctic (Piersma *et al.* 1990; Fig. 3). For example, little or no correlation was found between spring temperatures at staging areas in western

FIG. 3. Arrival on the tundra is timed to fit average snowmelt and appearance of sufficient invertebrate food. Some birds still carry a surplus of body stores as an insurance against spells of poor weather upon arrival and to enable transformation of organs, so that the birds can change from 'migration machines' to 'breeding machines'. Red knots at Cape Sterlegova, Taimyr, Siberia, 15 June 1994. Photo: Jan van de Kam.

Europe and initial observation dates on or close to the breeding grounds in subarctic Iceland and in High Arctic Greenland, where the birds must cross hundreds of kilometers of open sea or sea ice *en route* (Meltofte 1985, Boyd and Petersen 2006). Arrivals in Iceland became earlier in the first half of the 20th century as temperatures in Iceland increased, but changed little in the second half, when Icelandic temperatures decreased slightly. Arrivals of the earliest arriving birds (hereafter "pioneers") were delayed after winters in which the North Atlantic Oscillation index had been positive and high, and in springs when westerly or cyclonic systems were prevalent over Ireland and Scotland (Boyd and Petersen 2006).

In the outer Yukon-Kuskokwim Delta of Alaska, where snow and ice persist much longer than just 100-200 km inland, first observation dates of nine out of 14 species correlated with spring temperatures, snow cover, and river break up, but this was the case for only one out of five species in the inner delta (B. McCaffery, unpubl.). The nine species showing correlation with spring progress in the outer delta were all local breeders, while three of the remaining species were either fully or predominantly passage migrants. Early arriving species tended to arrive more synchronously and their arrival was more strongly correlated with local environmental conditions.

In the Yukon-Kuskokwim Delta no temporal trends in first arrival dates (i.e. of pioneers) were found in 17 shorebird species during 1977-2003 (B. McCaffery, unpubl.), despite a significant spring warming trend over that interval. Similarly, on the other side of the Bering Strait, local breeders have not exhibited a change in arrival dates either, despite a possible climatic amelioration (P.S. Tomkovich, unpubl.).

In the Siberian and Canadian Arctic, shorebirds sometimes stop short of the breeding grounds if they meet unfavorable conditions (Ganter and Boyd 2000, Schekkerman *et al.* 2004, L. Nguyen, pers. comm., Trent University, 2002-2004). Late spring melt may even temporarily shift the breeding distribution in opportunistic species (see further under 'Population densities and distribution' below). In years with late snowmelt, shorebirds arrived one or two weeks later and over a more extended period in the Siberian and Canadian Arctic (Syroechkovski and Lappo 1994, Tomkovich *et al.* 1994, Tomkovich 1995, Tomkovich and Soloviev 1996, E. Nol, unpubl.). In southwest Taimyr, Russia, temporary staging of shorebirds breeding farther North may occur, followed by departure in response to temperature increases (Schekkerman *et al.* 2004).

Pre-nesting period and egg-laying

Arctic shorebirds must possess surplus nutrient and energy stores when they arrive on the breeding grounds: these stores are accumulated at stopover areas (Piersma *et al.* 1999), and not only provide insurance against periods of inclement weather upon arrival, but also appear to facilitate rebuilding of digestive and other organs after the long flight in preparation for breeding (Morrison and Hobson 2004, Morrison *et al.* 2005). This means that shorebirds could face problems if they encounter unfavorable winds or weather *en route*, resulting in depletion of body stores accumulated before take off, or if they are unable to accumulate adequate stores at the final spring stopover site before departure for the Arctic (Morrison 2006). Evidence of mass mortality exists from both the Nearctic and the Palearctic, when shorebirds met snowstorms or other severe weather upon or after arrival (Morrison 1975, Boyd 1992, Pozdnyakov 1997, Lyngs 2003). Under such conditions, reverse migration has been observed (Meltofte 1985, Syroechkovski and Lappo 1994, Ganter and Boyd 2000).

In the Siberian Arctic, body mass of late arriving sandpipers *Calidris* spp. in unfavorable years was significantly reduced (Soloviev and Tomkovich 1997). At Alert, Canada in 1999, post-arrival masses of red knots *Calidris canutus* were lower than the long term mean, and extensive early season snow cover both there and in Northeast Greenland resulted in many shorebirds foregoing breeding or breeding later (Meltofte 2000, Morrison *et al.* 2005). Red knots departing from Iceland in better than average condition in the early 1970s on their way to the High Arctic breeding grounds in Greenland and Canada were more likely to survive the colder summers that occurred in subsequent years than those that had left in average condition (Morrison 2006, Morrison *et al.* 2007). Reduced refueling rates in red knots at the last stopover site in Delaware Bay, New Jersey, prior to the flight to the tundra breeding grounds led to reduced body condition at departure and were correlated with low subsequent survival, both at the individual and population level (Baker *et al.* 2004).

Generally, the duration of the total egg-laying period decreases from the south to the north in shorebirds (Väisänen 1977). In some sub- and Low Arctic areas, egg-laying may be initiated as early as mid May (e.g. western Alaska), but in most of the subarctic and the Arctic egg-laying typically begins after 1 June, and the last (replacement) clutches are initiated in late June or early July (Meltofte 1985, Morozov and Tomkovich 1988, Gratto-Trevor 1992, Tomkovich et al. 1994, Nol et al. 1997, Sandercock et al. 1999). The termination of egg-laying is probably dictated by the need of adults to arrive at temperate and tropical non-breeding areas, when food is at its summer peak there (Schneider and Harrington 1981), to complete prebasic molt as early as possible (for those wintering in temperate areas), and for the young to have sufficient time for development before the first frost occurs on the tundra (Meltofte 1985, Tomkovich and Soloviev 2001). Predator avoidance may also play a role, in that early departure can result in avoidance of the peak migration of avian predators (Lank et al. 2003).

Because Arctic shorebirds obtain almost all the resources for egg-formation on the breeding grounds (documented in 10 species at 13 Arctic study sites; Klaassen et al. 2001, Morrison and Hobson 2004), they typically need a period of at least 5-8 days after arrival before the first eggs are laid, and a strong correlation has been frequently documented between timing of arrival and egg-laying (Schamel and Tracy 1987 and unpubl., Schamel et al. 2002, Schekkerman et al. 2004, B. McCaffery, unpubl.). This timing is consistent with the minimum time required for egg formation in shorebirds (Roudybush et al. 1979), but shorebirds in High Arctic locations may require some additional time for physical transformation from migration to breeding condition (Morrison et al. 2005). In phalaropes *Phalaropus* spp., an apparent exception to the pattern of 'income' breeding is seen, because adults arrive with sufficient body stores derived from their marine staging areas or already paired (Mayfield 1979, Schamel and Tracy 1987). Thus, in these species the time between arrival and egg-laying can be as short as two days. This short period is also facilitated by their proportionately smaller eggs (Ross 1979).

Initiation of egg-laying (first and median laying dates) at individual study sites across the Arctic and subarctic varied interannually by up to 2-3 weeks, depending on weather and snowmelt (Meltofte 1985, Tomkovich 1988, Tomkovich et al. 1994, Troy 1996, Nol et al. 1997, Tomkovich and Soloviev 2001, Schekkerman et al. 2004, Soloviev et al. 2005, C.L. Gratto-Trevor, unpubl., B. McCaffery, unpubl., R.I.G. Morrison, unpubl., D. Schamel and D.M. Tracy, unpubl.;

FIG. 4. During the first days on the tundra, feeding areas are often limited by snow cover, invertebrate food densities are often poor, but still, the females need to obtain local resources for egg production. In years with late snowmelt and/or cold weather, egg-laying may be delayed by up to 2-3 weeks. Purple sandpipers at Cape Sterlegova, Taimyr, Siberia, 13 June 1994. Photo: Jan van de Kam.

Fig. 4). By contrast, in Low Arctic northern Norway, where influence from the Gulf Stream reduces interannual differences in temperature and snow cover, first laying dates of dunlins *Calidris alpina* varied by only 10 days in 14 years of study, while mean laying dates varied by only five days (H.-U. Rösner and B. Ganter, unpubl.).

Because large differences in snow and temperature regimes exist between valleys only a few hundred kilometers apart in mountainous High Arctic Greenland and the Canadian High Arctic Archipelago, differences in egg-laying dates in these regions match differences found over much larger areas in the lowlands of the remaining North American and Siberian Arctic (Green *et al.* 1977, Meltofte 1985, Holmgren *et al.* 2001). Furthermore, spring snow cover decreases from south to north in High Arctic Greenland and in the Canadian Arctic Archipelago. The result is that shorebirds breed earlier in the northernmost lands in the World, Peary Land and northern Ellesmere Island, than in many other parts of the Arctic (Meltofte 1976, R.I.G. Morrison, unpubl.). Similarly, nesting of semipalmated sandpipers *Calidris pusilla* occurs at the same time in Alaska and northern Manitoba, even though the Alaskan study site is much farther north (Gratto and Cooke 1987). This illustrates that it is not the height of the sun alone (i.e. latitude) or similarly fixed clues that determine the onset of egg-laying, but a combination of environmental factors such as snow cover, temperature, and food availability.

At Zackenberg, Northeast Greenland, food availability during egg-formation was found to be the prime determinant of initiation of egg-laying (Meltofte *et al.* 2006b). However, in years with less than 25% snow-free land in early spring, snow cover appeared to be the most important factor. This agrees with several studies on temperate shorebirds and other birds, where timing of egg-laying early in the season is molded by seasonal changes in food availability (Högstedt 1974, Drent and Daan 1980, Lank *et al.* 1985, Drent *et al.* 2003).

As another indication of possible food limitation during egg-laying, western sandpipers *Calidris mauri* and red-necked phalaropes *Phalaropus lobatus* in Alaska had laying intervals between the eggs in a clutch that were up to twice as long in early clutches as in later ones (Schamel 2000, D.R. Ruthrauff and B. McCaffery, unpubl.). Laying intervals were also relatively longer in Temminck's stint *Calidris temminckii* under severe weather conditions at the northern limit of their breeding range (Tomkovich 1988).

Egg-laying may be disrupted or nests abandoned under conditions of unusually cold temperatures, heavy snowfall or cold rain (Hildén 1979, Meltofte 1985, 2003, B. McCaffery, unpubl., D. Schamel and D.M. Tracy, unpubl., see further in chapter below on 'Energetic constraints and nest abandonment during incubation'). During such spells of inclement weather, shorebirds may gather into flocks, and reverse migration has been observed (Meltofte 1985, Tomkovich 1994, Å. Lindström, University of Lund, pers. comm. 2003).

Although absence of breeding over an extensive geographical area has never been documented among Arctic shorebirds, varying proportions of local populations may refrain from breeding in particularly unfavorable years (Mayfield 1978, Gratto-Trevor 1991, Tomkovich *et al.* 1994, Troy 1996, Meltofte 2000, E. Nol, unpubl., J.R. Jehl, Smithsonian Institute, pers. com. 2000). A late spring and very low temperatures in 1992 following the 1991 eruption of Mount Pinatubo in the Philippines resulted in widespread abandonment of breeding particularly in waterfowl, but to some extent even in shorebirds (Ganter and Boyd 2000). Low temperatures and late snow during early and mid June 2004 again resulted in extensive reductions (over 50% of long-term average number of breeding pairs) in breeding populations of shorebirds in the western Hudson Bay region of the Canadian subarctic (E. Nol, unpubl.). In both years, shorebirds were less uniformly affected than Arctic geese.

A shorter period of total egg-laying was documented in late seasons in several studies (Green *et al.* 1977, Schamel *et al.* 2002, 2003, Schekkerman *et al.* 2004, Meltofte *et al.* 2006b, B. McCaffery, unpubl., M.Y. Soloviev and V.V. Golovnyuk, unpubl.), probably because 1 July may be regarded as a general cut-off date for egg-laying with little prospect of success in later clutches (Tomkovich 1988, Gratto-Trevor 1992, Tulp *et al.* 2000, Tomkovich and Soloviev 2001, Graham 2004).

Arctic shorebirds often spend more than 50% of their time foraging during the pre-laying and laying periods, and time spent foraging during this phase frequently exceeds that during other phases of the breeding season supporting the notion that Arctic shorebirds potentially could experience food stress during the pre-breeding period. In a favorable season at Zackenberg, Greenland, four shorebird species used 75-92% of daytime hours to feed during pre-nesting, whereas off-duty incubating birds used only about half this time (Meltofte and Lahrmann 2006). Similarly, Ashkenazie and Safriel (1979) found that female semipalmated sandpipers fed 60-70% of the time during pre-laying and laying in northernmost Alaska, only exceeded by the pre-migratory fattening period (see below). In the severe breeding environment of the High Arctic desert of Franz-Josef Land, Russia, purple sandpipers *Calidris maritima* fed through almost all the daytime hours (100% in females and 92% in males) during egg-laying (Tomkovich 1985). In Taimyr, Siberia, Hötker (1995) found that feeding took up only 30% to 76% of the time during pre-nesting in five shorebird species: male black-bellied plovers *Pluvialis squatarola* fed less than half the pre-nesting time, while female black-bellied plovers and the other species all spent more than 56% of their time feeding. Similarly, pre-nesting female Eurasian golden-plovers *Pluvialis apricaria* in the low-alpine Norwegian mountains used about 60-90% of their time feeding, or 1.5 times as much as males, and in both sexes more than at any other part of the breeding season (Byrkjedal 1985).

In contrast to these findings, red knots and ruddy turnstones *Arenaria interpres* showed reduced feeding during the first week after arrival on their north Ellesmere Island, Canada, breeding grounds, especially during periods of cold weather, and they spent much of their day resting after their long flight from Iceland (Morrison and Davidson 1990, Davidson and Morrison 1992, see also Parmelee and MacDonald 1960). Schwilch *et al.* (2002) suggested shorebirds may require a rest/recovery period after a long migration, and it is also less expensive energetically to roost and shelter during periods of poor weather than to attempt foraging at a time when little food is available. In addition, during the first week after arrival, energy stores brought to the breeding grounds from Iceland may be used for re-growth of various organs, which were reduced prior to or during flight (Morrison *et al.* 2005). Energy stores brought to the breeding grounds may thus serve to provide nutrients for body transformations as well as to provide energy for survival, thus negating the necessity for periods of heavy feeding at least shortly after arrival.

Very few long-term data are available on trends in timing of egg-laying during recent decades of climate amelioration in the Arctic. Schamel *et al.* (1999) found no difference over a two-decade comparison in a range of species at Cape Espenberg, Alaska. Similarly, time of peak and median nest initiations of western sandpipers on the Yukon-Kuskokwim Delta did not change between 1966-1968 and 1998-2003 (Holmes 1972, B. McCaffery, unpubl.). However, a significant trend towards earlier breeding during 1994-2003 was found in all shorebird species at lower Khatanga River, southeastern Taimyr (M.Y. Soloviev and V.V. Golovnyuk, unpubl.), a change that was accompanied by a significant increase in early June temperatures (during pre-nesting 31 May – 14 June). During these years, no significant trends were found for dates of snowmelt, or precipitation in the pre-nesting and incubation periods.

Clutch size and egg volume

Arctic shorebirds normally lay a clutch of four eggs, but many studies have found increased occurrence of clutches with three or two eggs in late breeding seasons and among late or replacement clutches (Meltofte *et al.* 1981, 2006b, Tomkovich 1991, Nol *et al.* 1997, Sandercock *et al.* 1999, Meltofte 2000, 2003, C.L. Gratto-Trevor, unpubl., H.-U. Rösner and B. Ganter, unpubl., M.Y. Soloviev and V.V. Golovnyuk, unpubl., see further in Sandercock *et al.* 1999, Schamel *et al.* 2002, and Schekkerman *et al.* 2004; Fig. 5).

Egg volumes of shorebirds are generally smallest in High Arctic and continental areas, and increase towards maritime areas in the same species (Väisänen 1977) possibly reflecting productivity gradients. A few studies have found that egg volumes were reduced in cold or late breeding seasons and among late or replacement clutches (western sandpipers, Sandercock *et al.* 1999; dunlin, Schamel *et al.* 2002; ruddy turnstones, R.I.G. Morrison, unpubl.), although late clutches had increased egg volume in red-necked phalaropes and western sandpipers at Cape Espenberg, Alaska (Schamel 1999, 2000). No interannual variability was found in egg volumes in maritime Low Arctic breeding dunlins during 14 years of study in northernmost Norway (H.-U. Rösner and B. Ganter, unpubl.), and egg volume in clutches of semipalmated plovers *Charadrius semipalmatus* that laid eggs in the late and cold breeding season of 1992 was similar to

FIG. 5. Shorebirds normally lay a clutch of four eggs, but in years with unfavorable conditions, clutch size is often reduced to three or even two eggs. Across the Arctic, 1 July is about the last date for egg-laying, which means that opportunities for re-nesting after loss of the first clutch are much reduced in late seasons. Sanderling on Rowley Island, Canada, June 1990. Photo: Jan van de Kam.

egg volume in other less cold years (Nol et al. 1997).

Energetic constraints and nest abandonment during incubation

Ambient weather conditions have major effects on levels of energy expenditure in Arctic-breeding shorebirds. The metabolic rate of Arctic shorebirds is highest during summer in the North, and shorebirds breeding in the extreme High Arctic expend about twice as much daily energy as birds incubating in a temperate climate (Lindström and Klaassen 2003, Piersma et al. 2003). The high costs of living do not appear to be due to the energetic cost of heating eggs (nests are usually placed in sheltered sites, and nest cups are often well-insulated, but see Andreev 1999, Reid et al. 2002). Instead, they appear to be due to costs of being active under cold and windy conditions, especially feeding in exposed habitats (Piersma et al. 2003). Body stores of incubating little stints *Calidris minuta* increased with latitude in the Eurasian Arctic (Tulp et al. 2002), and Cartar and Morrison (2005) showed that shorebirds living in metabolically more costly parts of the Canadian Arctic showed reduced tarsus length, apparently an evolutionary adaptation for reducing metabolic costs. Even in the mild Low Arctic Yukon-Kuskokwim Delta of Alaska, shorebirds seek shelter in the lee of hummocks during windy off duty times, probably to reduce energy expenditure (B. McCaffery, unpubl.).

In one comparison, energy expenditure of red knots was about 20-30% higher in cool High Arctic Siberia than in more moderate breeding season temperatures of High Arctic Canada (Piersma 2002). In another comparison, thermostatic costs of ruddy turnstones at Alert on northern Ellesmere Island were similar to those on Rowley Island in the Foxe Basin, some 1700 km to the south in Canada (Piersma and Morrison 1994). Although Alert was colder, conditions on Rowley Island were windier, leading to similar thermostatic costs owing to the wind-chill factor. Because Arctic shorebirds need to obtain energy for their own maintenance during incubation, when they have only 50% or less of their time available for feeding, adverse weather conditions during incubation can potentially affect both adult survival and breeding success (Cartar and Montgomerie 1987).

In shorebird species that employ uniparental incubation, nest attendance occurs for 75-85% of available time. This compares to <50% of the time for biparental incubators. By sharing incubation, each parent in a biparental species has up to 12 hours per day for foraging, while, in uniparental species, the time available is between 3.5 and 6 hours daily (Norton 1972, Erckmann 1981, Kondratyev 1982, Cartar and Montgomerie 1987, Tulp and Schekkerman 2006). The higher 'energetic stress' for a uniparental incubator, the little stint, was reflected in a drop in body mass when temperature was low for several days, indicating depletion of stores. Body mass of biparental dunlins showed no such change under the same conditions (Tulp and Schekkerman 2006), and weight loss of birds trapped on the nest after cold days was observed in only one of 10 years in female biparental semipalmated plovers (Graham 2004). MacLean (1969, cited in Norton 1972) found increased frequency and duration of nest absences in uniparental pectoral sandpipers *Calidris melanotos* under adverse weather conditions. In white-rumped sandpipers *Calidris fuscicollis*, another uniparental incubator, duration of nest absences increased with ambient temperature, whereas frequency decreased (Cartar and Montgomerie 1987). Uniparental red-necked phalaropes had prolonged egg-laying intervals, and also prolonged incubation period among the early breeding segment of the population, suggesting energetic limitations for the adults (Schamel 2000). Similarly, uniparental Temminck's stints showed longer total incubation periods under severe conditions owing to temporary absence from the nest (Hildén 1965, Tomkovich 1988). This may be the reason why uniparental species typically breed later than biparental species (Whitfield and Tomkovich 1996).

In situations where incubators left their nests unattended during feeding as a result of poor weather, this rarely resulted in nest failure (Graham 2004, Schamel *et al.* 1999, Tulp and Schekkerman 2006, however see Erckmann 1981, for evidence of desertion). Massive nest desertions following heavy snowfalls have been documented occasionally, but some nests are able to survive even when almost totally snow covered (Hildén 1979, Meltofte 1979, 2003, Tomkovich 1988, Tomkovich *et al.* 1994, Tomkovich and Soloviev 2001, see also Norton 1972). During hatching, eggs and young are particularly vulnerable to cold weather, but by incubation behavior and vocal communication with the unhatched chick, parent birds are apparently able to delay hatching of the chicks by up to three days when environmental conditions are poor (Norton 1972, Kondratyev 1982, Tomkovich and Soloviev 2001).

Desertion of late nests has been found in several studies (Gratto-Trevor 1992, Tomkovich *et al.* 1994, Meltofte 2000, Tulp and Schekkerman 2006). Another climate-related cause of nest loss is flooding during heavy snowmelt or rain (Holmes 1966, Meltofte 1985, Handel and Gill 2001, A. Ronka, University of Oulu, Finland, pers. com. 2003). In a river delta site at subarctic La Pérouse Bay, Canada, melt of delta ice was a month later than average in 1983, but semipalmated sandpipers nested in normal numbers and at normal dates. During the late melt, although nests were not directly flooded, many pairs deserted, presumably because insect prey was unavailable in the floodwaters (Gratto *et al.* 1985).

Predation on eggs

Predation pressure on shorebird clutches varies widely regionally, interannually, and even within each nesting season with nest losses to predators ranging from close to 0% to near 100% (Ryabitsev *et al.* 1976, Mayfield 1978, Tomkovich *et al.* 1994, Sandercock 1998, Schamel *et al.* 1999, Ruthrauff 2002, McCaffery and Ruthrauff 2004a, Graham 2004, Hansen and Meltofte 2006, C.L. Gratto-Trevor, unpubl., R.I.G. Morrison, unpubl., M.Y. Soloviev and V.V. Golovnyuk, unpubl.).

Arctic-breeding shorebirds exhibit within-season variation in nest losses to predators. Some studies have demonstrated that earlier nests are more successful, as in spoon-billed sandpiper *Eurynorhynchus pygmeus* (Tomkovich 1995). In western sandpipers, nest survival was significantly higher in early clutches in only two out of six study years in Low Arctic Alaska, with no difference in the six years combined (B. McCaffery, unpubl). Nest success can also be lower in the early season, as in red-necked phalaropes in western

FIG. 6. Shorebirds lay their eggs on the ground, where they are vulnerable to predators. The arctic fox is the most important egg predator, and predation varies with fox density and the abundance of alternative prey, particularly lemmings. The result is that breeding success fluctuates considerably with the lemming cycle, often being close to nil in years after a lemming peak, where foxes are common and alternative prey is scarce, so that foxes turn to bird eggs instead. Ruddy turnstone on Rowley Island, Canada, June 1990. Photo: Jan van de Kam.

Hudson Bay, Canada (Reynolds 1987). At this site, early nesters took longer to complete egg-laying and incubation, exposing nests to predators for a longer time. In addition, predators may have smaller areas of suitable breeding habitat to search early in the season before snowmelt has been completed (see below).

In general, Arctic-nesting shorebirds breed more successfully in years with early breeding. Sandercock (1998) found significantly higher nest survival in western sandpipers and semipalmated sandpipers in early seasons, as did Schamel et al. (2003) in western sandpipers and Nol et al. (1997) in semipalmated plovers. The same pattern was found in semipalmated sandpipers at La Pérouse Bay, western Hudson Bay, but the correlation at that study site may be confounded by a concomitant pattern in microtine rodent numbers (C.L. Gratto-Trevor, unpubl., see below).

The most important egg predator in most parts of the Arctic is the arctic fox *Alopex lagopus*, and preda-

tion is highly influenced by fox activity and availability of other prey, particularly lemmings *Dicrostonyx* spp. and *Lemmus* spp. (Fig. 6). In Gamvik, northern Norway, with neither arctic foxes nor pronounced rodent fluctuations, dunlin nest survival was uniformly high across years (H.-U. Rösner and B. Ganter, unpubl.). Lemming cycles did not appear to have influenced nest success of semipalmated plover over 13 years of monitoring along the south-western Hudson Bay coast, as annual variation in nest success was low (between 52% and 73%, E. Nol, unpubl.). Microtine cycle and predation rates on semipalmated sandpipers at nearby La Pérouse Bay were negatively correlated over eight years of study. Here, the three years with the lowest predation on semipalmated sandpiper nests were the three earliest in terms of median date of egg-laying, and the three with highest numbers of microtines (C.L. Gratto-Trevor, unpubl.). Several studies have indicated that egg predation tends to be low in rodent rich years and high in years after a lemming peak, when the number of foxes may also be high (Summers and Underhill 1987, Underhill et al. 1993, Gratto-Trevor 1994, Troy 1996, Smith et al. 2007). Cycles in shorebird productivity detected on the non-breeding grounds have been linked with lemming cycles on the breeding grounds (Summers et al. 1998).

Krebs et al. (2002) suggested that weather was a major factor causing synchrony in Arctic lemming populations, and weather such as late spring melt, lack of snow, freezing rain and severe cold appears to influence the effects of the well-defined lemming cycles that occur at Alert (R.I.G. Morrison, unpubl.). Because rodent fluctuations are particularly strong in snow-rich areas (Stenseth and Ims 1993), this may involve a large scale climate impact on predation pressure on shorebird nests.

Increased predation risk during egg-laying in areas or years with extensive spring snow cover may be a contributing factor in the correlation between snow cover and egg-laying (Byrkjedal 1980). For example, Meltofte et al. (1981) found significantly higher fox predation on ruddy turnstone clutches in early than in late (replacement) clutches in a snow-rich (93% on 10 June) area in High Arctic Greenland in spite of large numbers of lemmings that year. Similarly, in seasons with heavy snow in the High Arctic part of Taimyr, birds start nesting when snow-free areas are limited in size and often resemble chains of snow-free patches on higher elevation patches of tundra. In such situations it is easy to see tracks of arctic foxes proceeding from one patch to another, and this coincides with mass disappearance of early eggs (P.S. Tomkovich, unpubl.). By contrast, egg predation was low early in a season at Medusa Bay, Siberia, when lemmings were forced out of their nests during snowmelt; predation increased markedly after the lemmings had occupied their summer burrows (Schekkerman et al. 2004). Prey-switching by predators may thus modify or obscure effects of snow cover on vulnerability of nests to depredation both between and within seasons.

Another climate impact relates to the possibilities for re-nesting after depredation of the initial clutch, so that egg-laying delayed by late snowmelt or poor food conditions results in less time for re-nesting before the end of the laying season (see above). For example, in a subarctic population of semipalmated sandpipers at La Pérouse Bay, Canada, none re-nested in late seasons, and there were few opportunities for re-nesting, as nests initiated after 1 July are usually deserted. Most re-nesting occurred in early seasons, where 47% of those losing nests before 26 June re-nested (Gratto-Trevor 1992 and unpubl.). A similar situation was found in sanderling *Calidris alba* on High Arctic northern Taimyr, where one third of the population may attempt to produce second clutches under the double-clutch breeding system, while in late seasons virtually no second clutches were laid (Tomkovich and Soloviev 2001). In the Low Arctic, on the Yukon-Kuskokwim Delta, western sandpipers re-nested in both early and late years, but the frequency of re-nesting was twice as high in the earliest year relative to the latest, and there was a significant linear relationship between median nest initiation date and the proportion of pairs re-nesting (B. McCaffery, unpubl.).

Chick-rearing

Arctic shorebird chicks are hypothesized to hatch around the time that insect prey abundance on the tundra is maximal (Hurd and Pitelka 1954, Holmes 1966, Nettleship 1973, 1974), but owing to spring weather and snow cover (see above), the extent to which there is a match does vary (Fig. 7). Growth rates of chicks were correlated with temperature and/or arthropod activity in all Siberian species studied to date (Schekkerman et al. 1998, 2003a, 2004, Tulp and Schekkerman in press) and proportion of time feeding was strongly related to ambient temperatures in American golden-plovers *Pluvialis dominica* (Krijgsveld et al. 2003). Three non-exclusive mechanisms underlie this. In cold weather (1) chicks expend more energy on thermoregulation at the expense of tissue formation, (2) small chicks require more parental brooding and thus have less time available for foraging, and (3) foraging success is reduced due to lower arthropod surface activity. In red knot chicks, arthropod activity explained variation in growth rate better than weather alone (Schekkerman et al. 2003a). On the Yukon-Kuskokwim Delta, in warm, dry years, black turnstone *Arenaria melanocephala* chicks achieved an average body mass at 11-12 days of age that was similar to that reached in 20-21 days in cold, wet years (Handel and Gill 2001). In Gamvik, northern Norway, fledging age of dunlin chicks varied between 16 and 19 days among 14 study years. This variation was most likely related to arthropod availability, and fledging date appears less variable at this Atlantic Low Arctic site than at other Arctic locations (H.-U. Rösner and B. Ganter, unpubl.).

On Taimyr, Siberia, activity of surface-dwelling invertebrates (the main food of shorebird chicks) was measured by pitfall trapping, and showed a very high weather-dependence superimposed on a unimodal seasonal pattern (Schekkerman et al. 2003a, Tulp and Schekkerman in press). Low temperature, rainfall, and strong winds drastically reduce arthropod activity. The amplitude of short-term weather-induced effects was as large as that of the seasonal pattern, and thus the vagaries of weather strongly influenced the temporal pattern of arthropod availability observed in a given year. This may obscure any relationship between the date of snowmelt and that of seasonal arthropod peak, and renders the timing of the latter highly unpredictable. Nevertheless, growth rate influenced fledging success. In little stints at Taimyr, broods that hatched on the declining flank of the arthropod peak in 2001 had a lower probability of being re-sighted subsequently than broods that hatched earlier and near the peak of arthropod abundance (Tulp and Schekkerman 2001). In curlew sandpipers *Calidris ferruginea*, a positive correlation was found between the proportion of juveniles in South African ringing samples during the Boreal winter and mean temperatures on the Taimyr Peninsula in the 10-day period that most chicks hatch (Schekkerman et al. 1998, see further below).

The correlations between arthropod activity and weather and date observed on Taimyr in 2000-2002 were used to estimate food availability for chicks from weather data over the past 30 years. The modeled date of peak insect activity ranged between 10 July and 1 August, and most often fell in the 2nd 10-day period of July. Based on the value of arthropod abundance at which growth rate becomes negatively affected, the probability that chicks encounter enough food on specific dates was calculated (Tulp and Schekkerman 2007). The probability that insect activity reached a level allowing 'normal' growth of chicks showed a flatter distribution, with values >0.2 between 5 and 31

FIG. 7. Arctic shorebird chicks hatch at a time when invertebrate food is usually abundant on the tundra, but periods with inclement weather may hamper chick growth to such an extent that it reduces chick survival. In general, early clutches hatch at a better time for chick growth than late clutches. Sanderling on Rowley Island, Canada, July 1990. Photo: Jan van de Kam.

July, but falling rapidly thereafter. Even during the period with the lowest variance in peak insect activity (20-27 July), this probability never exceeded 0.5 (Tulp and Schekkerman in press). Hatching dates of shorebird chicks in 2000-2002 nearly all fell within this period with reasonable probability of sufficient food, suggesting that shorebirds timed their breeding for an 'average year' (Myers and Pitelka 1979, Tulp and Schekkerman in press). Early springs led to the entire pre-fledging period falling within the period of peak insect activity, which may be important, as larger chicks require more energy than small ones. However, even in early years, insect availability may be such that late-hatched chicks suffer reduced growth and survival due to decreasing food availability. Moreover, a trend towards earlier dates of the insect peak was observed during the study period, with a c. 6-day difference between 1970 and 2002 (Tulp and Schekkerman in press).

A similar analysis of weather and arthropod data from Zackenberg in High Arctic Greenland indicated that shorebird chicks experienced a longer period of sufficient food availability during summer than on Taimyr (I. Tulp, unpubl., see also Green *et al.* 1977). This is related to the more continental and favorable weather at this site than in High Arctic Taimyr, where Tomkovich and Soloviev (2001) reported that "During all three [study] years snow storms occurred repeatedly during summer". For only one out of nine seasons at Zackenberg we found indications of food limitations in shorebird chicks due to inclement weather (Meltofte 1998). Still, there was a positive correlation between red knot and ruddy turnstone populations and July temperatures two years earlier (these two species takes at least two years to mature); suggesting that chick survival even here could vary significantly (Meltofte 2006).

As in Taimyr, reduced chick survival late in the season was found in western sandpipers in Alaska (Ruthrauff and McCaffery 2005), and unfledged chicks in late broods are sometimes left unattended by parents because adults simply depart (e.g. Morozov and Tomkovich 1988, Tomkovich *et al.* 1994, Neville 2002). In addition, there is the risk of severe weather events such as snow storms in July that can kill many chicks (Ryabitsev 1993, Meltofte 2001, Tomkovich *et al.* 1994, see also Tomkovich and Fokin 1983).

In addition to optimal timing of chick hatching and growth in relation to arthropod peak abundance in July, early breeding maximizes the length of the period available for build up of juvenile body stores before departure on their first migration (Fig. 8). In this context, the finding of Meissner (2004) that juvenile Siberian red knots staging on the Baltic coast of Poland had shorter wings and bills in two years with cold summers may be relevant. The building up of fat stores might be especially important in parts of the Arctic where juveniles must cross large expanses of ocean or fly over obstacles such as the Greenland icecap (2000 m a.s.l.). In Arctic Canada and Siberia, where for some species it is possible to migrate in small hops between coastal stopover sites, little pre-migratory fattening was found (Tulp and Schekkerman 2001 and unpubl., Lindström *et al.* 2002). However, at High Arctic Alert, northern Ellesmere Island, Canada, both adult and juvenile red knots and ruddy turnstones put on large amounts of fat prior to migration, indicating that they make a long-haul flight out of the Arctic (R.I.G. Morrison, unpubl.). It may also be noted that the peak in arthropod availability occurs not only during the peak chick-rearing season, but at a time when many adult shorebirds (principally females that have abandoned broods to the care of the male) are actively accumulating fat and other body stores before departure from the Arctic (R.I.G. Morrison, unpubl.).

On Taimyr, adults of all shorebird species had lower body mass during chick-rearing than during incubation, possibly because large energy stores were less necessary in the chick-tending period due to a lower incidence of cold spells, a two- to three-fold increase in time available for foraging and with maximum availability of arthropod food resources (Soloviev and Tomkovich 1997, Tulp *et al.* 2002, Tulp *et al.* 2007, R.I.G. Morrison, unpubl.). In addition it could even be advantageous to be lean because the costs of flight and terrestrial locomotion depend on body mass (Pennycuick, 1989; Bruinzeel *et al.*, 1999), and predation risk is expected to increase with the amount of reserve tissue (Lima 1986, Houston and McNamara 1993, Witter *et al.* 1994, Gosler *et al.* 1995). However, in semipalmated sandpipers in northernmost Alaska, where chick attendance and supposed pre-migratory fattening overlap, both males and females used about 80% of their time feeding (Ashkenazie and Safriel 1979).

FIG. 8. The earlier the chicks hatch, the more time they have to grow and develop before they have to leave the Arctic, where at high latitudes, winter can begin as early as September. Juvenile and adult red knots at Cape Sterlegova, Taimyr, 26 July 1994. Photo: Jan van de Kam.

Total juvenile production and recruitment to the breeding population

In the Arctic, breeding success as measured by juvenile production varies considerably. Among red knots from High Arctic Greenland/Canada, juvenile proportions on the Northwest European wintering grounds varied between 0.5% and 44% during 1969-1995, with most years ranging between about 10% and 35%: poor weather on the breeding grounds was associated with low production of juveniles - for instance, after the late and cold 1992 breeding season almost no juveniles were captured on the European wintering grounds (Boyd and Piersma 2001). Semipalmated plovers in subarctic Churchill, western Hudson Bay, produced no fledglings in either 2000 or 2004, two years with extreme low temperatures (E. Nol, unpubl.). Boyd and Piersma (2001) did not find significant correlations between juvenile numbers and breeding range summer temperatures in red knot, probably a result of the non-uniform nature of the Greenland-Canadian breeding grounds in spring snow cover and weather (see also Zöckler and Lysenko 2000). Again, in Low Arctic northernmost Norway there was comparatively little inter-annual variation in dunlin breeding success (the estimated maximum number of fledged chicks per breeding adult in the area varied between 0.83 and 1.39 in 14 years of study 1991-2004, H.-U. Rösner and B. Ganter, unpubl.).

In a preliminary analysis of counts of juvenile shorebirds made at two-weekly intervals during the period of southward migration at sites in the Maritime Provinces on the east coast of Canada between 1974 and 1998, juvenile proportions for a number of species were directly related to climatic conditions in parts of the Canadian Arctic used by the species for breeding (Morrison 2004). Correlational and principal components analyses showed that proportions of juveniles for many species were correlated with climate variables known to affect nesting (June) or brood-rearing (July) success in a positive (temperature) or negative (snow depth, wind, precipitation) manner. For instance, juvenile proportions for red knots were negatively correlated with June snow cover in the eastern Canadian Arctic, and for sanderling were positively correlated with June temperature in the western Canadian Arctic and negatively with July snow cover in the central Arctic. Similar relationships were found in other species (e.g., semipalmated sandpiper, black-bellied plover) with some exceptions (e.g., white-rumped sandpiper) (R.I.G. Morrison, unpubl.; see however McCaffery et al. 2006).

In the Siberian Arctic, conditions are more variable than in most other parts of the Arctic with juvenile production fluctuating from almost none to plentiful between years primarily related to rodent abundance (Ryabitsev et al. 1976, Summers and Underhill 1987, Underhill et al. 1993, Tomkovich et al. 1994). Hence, fluctuations in total juvenile numbers, juvenile proportions in ringing samples, or numbers of over-summering one-year-old shorebirds from breeding areas in the central parts of the Siberian tundra have indicated large and roughly three-yearly cyclic variation in productivity (e.g. Summers and Underhill 1987). The main source of this variability is predators such as arctic foxes and skuas (*Stercorarius* spp.), which apparently prefer to feed on lemmings, but switch to bird eggs and young when lemmings are scarce (see section on Predation on eggs).

Effects of weather on shorebird juvenile production in the Siberian Arctic were examined by correlating variation in the proportion of juveniles among non-breeding curlew sandpipers in South Africa over 18 years 1977-1994 with summer temperature records from the core breeding area on Taimyr (Schekkerman et al. 1998). After controlling for the predation-mediated effect of lemming abundance, breeding productivity (range 0-57% juveniles) was positively correlated with mean temperature in Taimyr during 11-20 July, the period when most young chicks are present on the tundra (see above). Weather thus seems to have effects on chick survival both widespread and large enough to be detected in the non-breeding areas, and the combination of (inferred) predation pressure, weather conditions and hence, food availability during the fledging period explains a large part of the variation in breeding productivity found in this species (77% plus 11%, respectively). Although correlations between productivity and temperature were examined for all 10-day periods in June-August, no others were significant including the pre-laying period. However, no data were available for date of snowmelt/snow depth at a certain date, as they are in Canada (see above).

Shorebird juvenile production in the eastern Siberian Arctic, examined by variation in the proportion of juveniles in Southeast Australia, was correlated with July temperature within breeding ranges in ruddy turnstone, curlew sandpiper, and red-necked stint *Calidris ruficollis*, and with the combined effect of June and July temperatures in sharp-tailed sandpiper *Calidris acuminata*. Effects of rodent abundance on shorebird breeding productivity were found only in red-necked stint and sharp-tailed sandpiper and were less pronounced compared to weather effects (Soloviev et al. 2006).

Ryabitsev (1993) found that breeding success in several site-tenacious species (Eurasian golden-plover, wood sandpiper *Tringa glareola* and Temminck's stint) was positively correlated with their nest density in the following year in subarctic Yamal, western Siberia, presumably through the recruitment of 1-year old birds into the local population, while significant relationships were not found in opportunistic species (little stint and ruff *Philomachus pugnax*) and in dunlin. This relationship in the site-tenacious species was explained by reduced recruitment to the breeding population in summers following seasons of breeding failure. Breeding densities of opportunistic species are subject to pronounced fluctuations due to redistribution of birds within the breeding range, and local effects of the previous reproductive success cannot be tracked on such background.

Similarly, Troy (1996) found that nesting densities of semipalmated sandpiper and dunlin – the most common site-tenacious species – fluctuated synchronously during an 11 year period at Prudhoe Bay in northern Low Arctic Alaska, and that fluctuations were related to hatching success two years before when recruits to the population were produced. These fluctuations in hatching success were related to predation by foxes reinforced by lemming crashes.

The post-breeding period of adults on the breeding grounds

Adult Arctic shorebirds appear to minimize the duration of their stay on the breeding grounds, so that they can return to non-breeding areas before invertebrate food resources decline (Schneider and Harrington 1981,

Meltofte 1985, 1996, Zwarts et al. 1992, Byrkjedal and Thompson 1998, van Gils et al. 2005a; Fig. 9). Furthermore, early departure may give the shorebirds a lead in relation to peak migration of avian predators (Lank et al. 2003). During autumn, shorebirds often complete primary molt and build up body stores for onward migrations or, for those who stay in temperate areas during winter, as an insurance against the unpredictability of weather conditions of the northern winter.

Failed breeders begin to form post-breeding flocks in mid or late June, soon followed by individuals who have left the care of the chicks to their mates (Meltofte 1985, Gratto-Trevor 1991, Syroechkovski and Lappo 1994, Tomkovich et al. 1994). Female semipalmated and western sandpipers desert their broods at an earlier age the later the brood hatches (Gratto-Trevor 1991, Neville 2002, Ruthrauff 2002), but even so, the result is that timing of autumn migration depends on timing of breeding and on breeding success (Syroechkovski and Lappo 1994, Tomkovich and Soloviev 1996, 2006, Blomqvist et al. 2002).

One exception is the dunlin, which frequently molts flight feathers, fully or partly, in the Arctic. In northern Alaska, for example, birds remain near the breeding grounds after breeding and complete primary molt there, and the molt increasingly overlaps with the breeding period to the north (Holmes 1971a, Kania 1990, Byrkjedal 1971, Tomkovich 1998, Holmgren et al. 2001). In many populations of this species, primary molt is triggered by onset of breeding. However, delayed clutch initiation in late seasons results in increased molt rate and completion of the molt about the same time in early August as in 'normal' seasons (Soloviev and Pronin 1998). Interestingly, in Gamvik, northern Norway, it is only a small proportion of the one year old breeding Dunlin who start primary molt there and none of the older ones (H.-U. Rösner and B. Ganter, unpubl.). Some populations of purple sandpipers also have a short, rapid molt on the breeding grounds before moving to the wintering grounds (Morrison 1976, 1984, Cramp and Simmons 1983).

FIG. 9. Adults of most species of shorebirds appear to leave the Arctic as early as possible to be able to go to the temperate and tropical non-breeding areas as early in the summer / autumn as possible. This has the advantage that they arrive when invertebrate food is at a maximum, and that they can commence the molt of flight feathers early in the season, before winter begins in temperate areas. The earlier they can breed, the earlier they can leave. Dunlins at Vatnajökull, Iceland, June 1996. Photo: Jan van de Kam.

During the post-breeding period, adult Arctic shorebirds, which must cross geographical barriers such as open sea (e.g. Nebel et al. 2000, Gill et al. 2005), build up body stores for the return flight to temperate and tropical non-breeding areas. Pre-migratory fattening primarily takes place during July-August, when food for adults is often plentiful along pond and lake shores, and on adjacent coasts – though it may already be declining on the tundra proper (cf. Holmes 1966, Holmes and Pitelka 1968, MacLean and Pitelka 1971, Nettleship 1973, Schekkerman and van Roomen 1995, Tulp et al. 1998, Tulp and Schekkerman in press).

Adult red knots passing through the Alert area, High Arctic Ellesmere Island, accumulate large body stores before departure (R.I.G. Morrison, unpubl., see above), and at Zackenberg, post-breeding adults (and juveniles) of four shorebird species used 75-88% of their day-time feeding, or largely the same as during pre-nesting and significantly more than during breeding proper (Meltofte and Lahrmann 2006). Similarly, semipalmated sandpipers in northernmost Alaska used about 80% of their time feeding during supposed pre-migratory fattening (Ashkenazie and Safriel 1979).

By contrast, adult (and juvenile) little stints, dunlins, curlew sandpipers and ruddy turnstones departing from southwest Taimyr had only small fuel stores (Tulp and Schekkerman 2001, in press). Body masses of departing birds were generally lower than during incubation, or even than upon arrival – with the exception of some adult curlew sandpipers and little stints. The general rule for these smaller species seemed to be to leave Taimyr at low mass, probably in small hops until better feeding sites were reached farther south/west along the migratory route (see also Lindström 1998, Lindström et al. 2002). The same pattern (i.e., limited or no obvious pre-migratory fattening) seems to hold for several populations of Calidris sandpipers in the middle parts of the North American Arctic, which appear to lack major geographical barriers at the northern end of their fall migration routes (Pitelka 1959, Yarbrough 1970, Jehl 1979).

Adult survival and site tenacity on the breeding grounds

Little information exists on adult survival during the breeding period. Generally, relative to their size, shorebirds are long-lived birds often with an annual survival of 70-90% and a very high, occasionally even complete, site tenacity (Boyd 1962, Evans and Pienkowski 1984, Evans 1991, Goede 1993, Sandercock and Gratto-Trevor 1997, Sandercock 2003, H.-U. Rösner and B. Ganter, unpubl.). As mentioned above, excessive mortality has been described in years with severe weather upon arrival, but otherwise there are few records of weather induced mortality. It is quite possible that in general most mortality in Arctic shorebirds occurs either during migration or at the staging and non-breeding quarters. However, in the cold summers of 1972, 1974 and 1992, the apparent mortality in Nearctic red knots was so high (and reproduction so poor) that it reduced the British wintering population by 21%, 24%, and 19%, respectively (Boyd and Piersma 2001), and was reflected by the exceptionally large number of band recoveries on the breeding grounds in Greenland (Lyngs 2003).

In semipalmated plovers at subarctic Churchill, Canada, where survival estimates for 11 years based on mark-recapture of breeding adults varied between 67% and 81% among years, adult survivorship was negatively correlated with the number of June days with sub-zero temperatures and positively correlated with breeding success (E. Nol, D.S. Badzinski and K. Graham, unpubl.). At nearby La Pérouse Bay, large numbers of semipalmated sandpipers deserted full-laid, non-flooded clutches after a very late melt in the delta in 1983, and only 6% returned the following year, compared to 30% from depredated nests and 67% from successful nests in other years. Many of the deserting birds had nested in the area for many years, so were unlikely to have emigrated, and as they were never seen again, they were more likely to have died (Gratto et al. 1985).

In the Americas, a dramatic decline in the population of rufa red knots observed between 2000 and 2002 coincided with a decrease in adult annual survival from 85% to 56% due to lack of food on the final spring staging areas (Baker et al. 2004, Morrison et al. 2004), the decrease in survival being enough to account for the observed decline. The islandica population of red knot underwent a marked decline during the early 1970s, which could be related to increased adult mortality due to poor spring weather on the High Arctic Greenland-Canadian breeding grounds (Boyd 1992, Lyngs 2003, Morrison 2006; see above).

Population densities, distribution and size

Shorebird breeding densities vary by more than a factor of 100 between the densest populations in Low Arctic parts of Alaska and Siberia, and the low densities of the High Arctic deserts of northern Greenland, the Canadian Archipelago and the Russian islands in the Arctic Ocean (Fig. 10). In prime habitat in Low Arctic Alaska, regional densities of up to 200 pairs of shorebirds have been found per km^2 – primarily calidridine sandpipers and phalaropes (McCaffery et al. 2002, B. McCaffery and J. Bart, unpubl.), with local densities of 250-750 pairs per km^2 (Holmes 1971b, Gill and Handel 1990, Schamel et al. 1999, McCaffery and Ruthrauff 2004b), and in north and north-eastern Siberia up to 100-150 pairs per km^2 have been found (Golovnyuk et al. 2004a, Schekkerman et al. 2004). In contrast, only a few pairs or even less are found per km^2 on Arctic desert (Meltofte 1985, Tomkovich 1985, Morrison 1997). More typical densities in shorebird habitat (excluding mountains, boulder fields etc.) in the Low Arctic are 15-100 pairs per km^2 (Ryabitsev and Alekseeva 1998, Jehl and Lin 2001, Brown et al. 2007, H.-U. Rösner and B. Ganter, unpubl., M.Y. Soloviev and V.V. Golovnyuk, unpubl.) and up to 5-50 pairs per km^2 in the southern High Arctic – mainly calidridine sandpipers and plovers (Meltofte 1985, 2006, Spiekman and Groen 1993, Underhill et al. 1993, Morrison 1997, Tulp et al. 1997 1998, Schekkerman et al. 2004, P.S. Tomkovich, unpubl.).

Holmes (1970) showed that dunlins defended territories five times as large at Point Barrow (close to the border between the High and the Low Arctic zones) compared to Low Arctic tundra 10° farther south in Alaska. He attributed this to differences in food density and predictability. Territory density ranged from 6 pairs/40 ha (15 pairs per km^2) in the north to 30 pairs/40 ha (75 pairs per km^2) in the south, where food

FIG. 10. Densities of breeding shorebirds may be 100 times as high in the productive sub- and Low Arctic areas as in the High Arctic desert. In the most productive areas in Alaska and northeastern Siberia, several hundred pairs may breed per km^2. A pair of bar-tailed godwits on Varanger, Norway, June 1992. Photo: Jan van de Kam.

density in preferred feeding habitat was 16 times higher than at Point Barrow, particularly in the early part of the breeding season. Similarly, shorebird breeding densities in High Arctic Greenland were best correlated with snow-free feeding habitat in early June (Meltofte, 1985).

Annual variation in local population densities depends in part on the biology of the individual species, with site-tenacious species often showing limited year-to-year variation, in contrast to 'opportunistic' species, which fluctuate widely according to local conditions (Pitelka et al. 1974, Pattie 1990, Ryabitsev 1993, Lappo 1996, Troy 1996, Ryabitsev and Alekseeva 1998, Golovnyuk et al. 2004a, Lappo and Tomkovich 2006, Meltofte 2006, Tomkovich and Soloviev 2006). In the Siberian Arctic, these opportunistic species may breed in high densities south of their 'normal' breeding range in years with late snowmelt or a cold spring (Rogacheva 1992, Ryabitsev and Alekseeva 1998, Golovnyuk et al. 2004a, Lappo and Tomkovich 2006). They may be able to move north for a new attempt after failed breeding in southern areas or for double-clutching (Tomkovich and Morozov 1983, Tomkovich 1988, Tulp et al. 2002, Tomkovich and Soloviev 2006, P.S. Tomkovich, unpubl.).

An effect on a site-tenacious species of early season temperatures was found at Churchill, western Hudson Bay, where the population of semipalmated plovers dropped from an average of 45 pairs to less than 27 in three years (1992, 2000 and 2004), each with average minimum daily air temperature below zero during the first 10 days of June (average number of pairs calculated for years 1988-2004, Graham 2004). Except for these three years, densities remained relatively stable. At Medusa Bay, Taimyr, a drastic reduction in density was only found in one out of six commonly breeding shorebirds species, the Pacific golden-plover *Pluvialis fulva*, in the late spring and summer of 2002 compared with early 2000 and 2001. Species showing no clear response included both site-tenacious ones and species with no site tenacity at all (Schekkerman et al. 2004).

Few data exist on long-term population changes. In general, modelling has indicated that shorebird populations are most sensitive to changes in adult mortality (Hitchcock and Gratto-Trevor 1997; see chapter on 'Adult survival and site tenacity on the breeding grounds'). However, under certain conditions recruitment may be relatively important (Atkinson et al. 2003, Boyd and Piersma 2001). For example, in the *islandica* knot population, trends in population size reflected long-term changes in both adult mortality rates and juvenile production, with suggestive evidence for density-dependent processes affecting reproductive success (Boyd and Piersma 2001). At Cape Espenberg, Alaska, a significant decrease in semipalmated sandpipers and western sandpipers took place from the 1970s to the 1990s, apparently as a result of increased predator abundance, but there was no significant decline in red-necked phalaropes or dunlins (Schamel et al. 1999). During the same period, the population of spoon-billed sandpipers declined about three-fold in Chukotka, easternmost Siberia (Tomkovich et al. 2002), and preliminary information indicates declines in populations of several other species at Belyaka Spit, Chukotsky Peninsula, belonging to the East Asian-Australasian flyway (P.S. Tomkovich, unpubl.). Declines of shorebirds in the Canadian Arctic have been reported near subarctic Churchill (Gratto-Trevor 1994, Jehl and Lin 2001), at the Low Arctic Rasmussen Lowlands (Gratto-Trevor et al. 1998, 2001, Johnston et al. 2000) and for some species in the High Arctic (Pattie 1990, Gould 1988, see also Morrison 2001).

Expansion of breeding ranges of several Arctic shorebirds also took place during the 20th century. Long-billed dowitcher *Limnodromus scolopaceus* expanded its breeding range by about 3000 km westward from Chukotka to western Taimyr in Siberia (Lappo 2000). Pintail snipe *Gallinago stenura* also expanded about 600 km westward into the European Low Arctic and subarctic (Morozov 1998). Sharp-tailed sandpiper was found recently at Taimyr, about 600 km west of its previous known breeding range, and numbers are still increasing there (Golovnyuk et al. 2004b). During the last three decades two Alaskan species, the semipalmated plover and the semipalmated sandpiper penetrated into Chukotsky Peninsula possibly due to climate amelioration, which allowed these American species to arrive and start breeding before Asian congenerics (Tomkovich and Syroechkovski 2005). In southern High Arctic Greenland, Eurasian golden-plover and whimbrel *Numenius phaeopus* have begun to breed during recent decades, possibly due to climate amelioration in the 20th century (Boertmann 1994). A 16-yr data set from the Truelove Lowlands of Devon Island, Canada (Pattie 1990), showed that the more southerly American golden-plover increased significantly after 1979 in a period (1980-1989) when average June temperatures were slightly higher (0.58°C versus -1.12°C) than in seven years between 1970 and 1979 (Environment Canada weather data). In parallel to these northward expansions of 'southern' species, red and red-necked phalaropes seem to be decreasing in the southern part of their range (Cramp and Simmons 1983, Whitfield 1995, Jehl and Lin 2001).

Range contractions are not known to us, but contractions are probably less well recorded.

Discussion

Arctic shorebirds spend most of the year on tidal coasts and other wetlands in temperate and tropical areas, but during the summer they expose themselves for a relatively few weeks to an often harsh Arctic environment to reproduce. Conditions on their breeding grounds vary dramatically both spatially, from apparently favorable environments in coastal northernmost Low Arctic Norway and some parts of the subarctic, to the harshness of the northernmost High Arctic tundras, and also temporally, from year to year in most areas.

Primary productivity is nearly 1000 times higher in Low Arctic shrub communities than in High Arctic desert (Jonasson *et al.* 2000), and this is the most likely explanation for the 100-fold higher shorebird breeding densities in certain sub- and Low Arctic areas than in High Arctic desert. Productivity (food) must be the overall governing factor in shorebird breeding density in the Arctic, but this will be regionally and locally moderated by long lasting snow cover, inclement weather, etc. Similarly, Henningsson and Alerstam (2005) found that shorebird species richness in the Arctic to a large degree is determined by primary production, the length of the snow-free period, the availability of migratory flyways, as well as the extent of tundra habitat during the last glaciation.

Our review has identified two periods of possible energetic bottlenecks: (1) the pre-nesting and egg-laying period all over the Arctic and (2) the chick growth period in large parts of the Arctic. Both aspects seem to involve that egg-laying as early as possible after arrival

FIG. 11. The most critical period during the shorebirds' stay in the Arctic seems to be the first days after arrival, when (1) food is limited and they transform their bodies from 'flying machines' to 'breeding machines', (2) they need surplus body stores to withstand spells of inclement weather, (3) they need local nutrients for egg production (in females), and (4) they need to initiate build-up of body stores for incubation. The result is that initiation of egg-laying varies by up to 2-3 weeks depending on food density and snow cover. Black-bellied Plover at Cape Sterlegova, Siberia, 20 June 1994. Photo: Jan van de Kam.

on the breeding grounds may be selected for in Arctic shorebirds in order to improve production of viable young, provide opportunities for re-nesting in the case of initial nest failure and facilitate early departure of adults and young.

After arrival and before egg-laying, Arctic shorebirds first must transform their bodies from 'flying machines' to 'breeding machines' (Fig. 11). Body stores accumulated on staging areas during migration and remaining after arrival on the breeding grounds may facilitate such physiological changes, while at the same time, body stores may also serve as an insurance against severe weather upon arrival (Piersma 1998, Morrison et al. 2005). In both respects, body stores accumulated at their final staging areas may be of great importance, and failure to acquire adequate stores before departure from the final spring stopover area may have severe survival consequences (Baker et al. 2004, Morrison 2006, Morrison et al. 2007). Stores acquired at high quality sites remotely from the nesting grounds themselves may thus play a key role in enabling shorebirds to breed early and successfully in the Arctic (Alerstam et al. 1986, Baker et al. 2004, van Gils et al. 2005b). Finally, after arrival shorebirds must acquire resources both for egg-laying (females), territory/mate defense (mostly males) and for incubation (most often both sexes) on the breeding grounds.

In large parts of the sub- and Low Arctic, snow is no problem in most years, while in parts of the Siberian Low Arctic and in the circumpolar High Arctic, 'sufficient' snow-free land must be available for feeding, nesting and spacing out of nests to reduce predation. Secondly, in all parts of the Arctic there must be enough food available for egg production, i.e. soil surface temperatures above freezing making invertebrates available (Chernov 1985, Hodkinson 2003).

Our review suggests that feeding conditions for chicks during pre-fledging influence production of juveniles, but that weather variation makes it very hard for a shorebird to predict the peak of insect emergence on a within-year timescale. This suggests that they do best by breeding as early as possible, so that as much

FIG. 12. Another critical period is the chick-rearing period, particularly in parts of the Arctic where inclement weather is common even in July. In all aspects of breeding, an early start seems beneficial. Little stint on Taimyr, Siberia, July 1992. Photo: Jan van de Kam.

DISCUSSION

as possible of the pre-fledging period falls within the period with a reasonable chance of finding sufficient food for the young to grow (Fig. 12).

Owing to large differences between regions, shorebirds are able to initiate egg-laying up to one month earlier in parts of the westernmost Nearctic compared to the eastern Canadian Arctic and parts of the Palearctic. A final date for laying around 1 July across the Arctic implies that the 'window' for re-nesting, in case of failure, is much longer in the early snow-free parts of the Arctic.

Taken together, feeding conditions during pre-nesting and egg-laying may be a strongly contributing factor in determining shorebird breeding densities and breeding performance in the Arctic. This is intensified in the High Arctic and parts of the Siberian Low Arctic, where up to 80-90% of the tundra may be snow covered during pre-nesting.

Across the Arctic, predation strongly influences breeding productivity. In the Siberian Arctic, lemmings are keystone species and any climate effects on their abundance or population dynamics may indirectly affect shorebird populations through predation. The role of lemmings in the eastern Canadian Arctic is unclear, but large annual fluctuations in lemming or other microtine populations suggest that similar dynamics operate there.

In spite of substantial differences demonstrated in this review between different parts of the Arctic, shorebird populations survive and reproduce – although in highly variable densities. Because we do not know to what extent pre-nesting feeding, chick feeding, or predation are intra- as well as inter-specifically density dependent, we cannot present firm conclusions on the effects of these factors in determining total population sizes. Are Arctic shorebird populations saturated on the breeding grounds, or are they more or less constantly kept below saturation by climate, predation, or other factors inside or outside the Arctic? (See Hale 1980, Evans and Pienkowski 1984, Troy 1996, van de Kam et al. 2004.) Population regulation may differ between species and populations, and even temporally. In addition, there may be transient inter-seasonal effects, so that a difficult breeding season results in increased mortality later in the year. Similarly, stressful non-breeding seasons may reduce body condition upon arrival in the Arctic and hence, affect breeding success (Schekkerman et al. 2003b, Baker et al. 2004) and survival (Morrison 2006, Morrison et al. 2007). Such cross-seasonal interactions await study.

Increases in summer temperatures in large parts of the Arctic during recent decades followed by earlier snowmelt and plant growth, at least in subarctic and Low Arctic areas (Foster 1989, Zhou et al. 2001, Dye 2002, Comiso 2003, Dye and Tucker 2003), has given rise to conflicting evaluations of possible effects on shorebird population sizes (Zöckler and Lysenko 2000 versus Meltofte et al. 2006a). The results presented in this review generally point to warmer spring and summer weather, at least initially, being beneficial to Arctic shorebirds particularly during the two phases of the breeding cycle which appear to be most critical (Fig. 13). Warmer winters with higher prey availability could also benefit populations wintering in temperate regions. Hence, warmer winters in western Europe during recent decades have made it possible for shorebirds to spend the non-breeding season farther north and east than previously (Austin et al. 2000, Rehfisch et al. 2004).

Scenarios for longer time-periods ahead are probably more complicated. The relationships between shorebird breeding performance and weather/temperature observed in studies performed within the range of variability seen in current climatic conditions may tell us little about effects over a longer time-scale and a larger amplitude of climate change. These are likely to involve more fundamental changes to Arctic ecosystems, of which the loss of breeding habitat is the most profound. In spite of the fact that Arctic shorebirds are resilient to great interannual variability, we do not know to what extent the birds are able to adapt to fast changing climatic conditions. Recent Arctic climate scenarios for the future (Kattsov et al. 2005) do not have a spatial or temporal resolution either for temperature, incoming radiation (cloud cover and thereby microclimate temperatures), precipitation (including duration of snow cover), or wind, nor for frequency and intensity of severe weather events, which would allow us to impute our findings into these models, but possibilities may improve in the near future (see Weber et al. 1998 for a first try). For the time being, it seems most useful to take a shortcut and look at macro-scale relationships between species and their environment. Because most Arctic shorebirds are largely confined to specific habitat zones within the Arctic, we must expect them to react to changes in the vegetation and climate occurring in these zones.

DISCUSSION

FIG. 13. Initially, global warming may benefit Arctic shorebirds because of earlier snowmelt and warmer summers with more stable food availability for adults and chicks, but in the longer term overgrowing of the tundra with shrubs and trees will probably reduce their breeding habitats significantly. Dunlin on Varanger, Norway, June 1995. Photo: Jan van de Kam.

A general expansion in subarctic shrub and Boreal forest is expected with increasing temperatures – and is already taking place (Myneni et al. 1997, Sturm et al. 2001, Stow et al. 2004, Goetz et al. 2005) – and this will reduce the breeding areas available to tundra shorebirds (Zöckler and Lysenko 2000). According to present climate scenarios, about half the Arctic may transform into subarctic shrub within this century, followed by forest expansion in the longer term (Huntley 1997, Solomon 1997, Callaghan et al. 2005). Another effect of global warming is the decrease in permafrost, lowering of the water table, and thus drying of marshes and ponds in the southern parts of the Arctic (Walsh et al. 2005). This type of habitat loss may have more immediate effects on shorebird populations here than the expansion of shrubs and trees. A continuation of warm summers may further lead to more and different predators, parasites and pathogens, etc. (e.g. Piersma 1997, Mouritsen and Poulin 2002, Freed et al. 2005, Barraclough 2006). This will most likely lead to a gradual decline in the suitability of the habitats for Arctic-breeding shorebirds. Northward expansion of Low Arctic and possibly temperate breeding shorebirds may also lead to interspecific competition for an increasingly limited supply of suitable nesting habitat.

As subarctic shrub expands northwards, the different Arctic plant zones are predicted to move northwards or disappear (Cramer 1997, Huntley 1997, Callaghan et al. 2005). This should be considered in relation to the Arctic presently being close to its minimum extent during the last 10,000 years, when viewed within a time scale of 150,000 years (Callaghan et al. 2004). Here, High Arctic shorebirds seem to be particularly at risk, because the High Arctic already constitutes a relatively limited area 'squeezed in' between the extensive Low Arctic biome and the Arctic Ocean (Lindström and Agrell 1999, Kaplan 2005), and some of these populations are already exposed to the most dramatic short-term fluctuations in weather (Table 1). Furthermore, the disappearance of dense ice cover on

DISCUSSION

large parts of the Arctic Ocean may cause the climate to become more maritime-dominated in the High Arctic – approaching present day Svalbard conditions, where few shorebirds breed (Norderhaug 1989). In this way, sanderling and red knot breeding habitat may not be reduced by only 5% and 15%, respectively, as proposed by Zöckler and Lysenko (2000), but with great probability by much more.

Conditions encountered by shorebirds in the non-breeding areas, together with wind systems during migration, could be altered by climate change and the expected sea level rise. Because most Arctic shorebirds live in intertidal areas outside the breeding season, and conditions there are fundamental for their ability to build up nutrient and energy stores for the long migrations to the breeding grounds and for their first days there, sea level rise affecting conditions on staging areas have the potential to dramatically alter shorebirds' abilities to breed successfully in the Arctic (Boyd and Madsen 1997, Lindström and Agrell 1999, Galbraith et al. 2002, Piersma and Lindström 2004, Morrison et al. 2007). For species dependent on inland spring staging areas, the anticipated drought in many temperate and subtropical areas would have the same effect (Boyd and Madsen 1997, McCarthy et al. 2001), and a 'mismatch' between the timing of migration and peak occurrence of invertebrate prey on staging areas could result from changes e.g. in spring phenology (Evans 1997, see also van Gils et al. 2005a). In this context it may be noted that opposite to species with culturally determined migration routes, shorebirds appear to be 'conservative migrants', i.e. among 57 documented cases of changed migration routes, no waders were found (Sutherland 1998). In addition, anthropogenic disturbances and destruction of shorebird non-breeding habitat, which continue at a high rate in many parts of the World, could possibly supersede and exacerbate effects of global climate change (Piersma and Lindström 2004).

Arctic-breeding shorebirds may be particularly vulnerable to climate change because they generally have low levels of intraspecific genetic variability compared with other birds. This low genetic variability has been shown by a variety of molecular techniques, including e.g. allozyme electrophoresis (Baker and Strauch 1988), mitochondrial DNA (mtDNA) sequencing (Baker et al. 1994, Wennerberg and Burke 2001, Wennerberg et al. 2002, Ottvall et al. 2004, Buehler and Baker 2005) and microsatellite (nuclear DNA) analysis (van Treuren et al. 1999, Wennerberg and Bensch 2001). High Arctic species like red knot (Buehler and Baker 2005) and curlew sandpiper (Wennerberg and Burke 2001) all have very low genetic variability, whereas e.g. the dunlin, which breeds in Low Arctic and temperate areas, shows more variation in mitochondrial DNA than any other shorebird studied so far (Wenink et al. 1993, Wenink et al. 1996, Wennerberg et al. 1999, Wennerberg 2001b). Microsatellites are less frequent in birds than in mammals (Primmer et al. 1997) and highly variable microsatellite loci have been difficult to identify in shorebirds. The few identified loci have also shown relatively low variability in Arctic species (van Treuren et al. 1999, Wennerberg and Bensch 2001, Thuman et al. 2002, Marthinsen et al. 2007). Similar to the results for mitochodrial DNA, the highest level of microsatellite variability published so far was found in a relatively southern breeding shorebird, the ruff (Thuman et al. 2002).

The low level of genetic variation in Arctic shorebirds is probably an effect of repeated population bottlenecks. Such bottleneck events are indicated both by the low level of variation within species (Baker and Strauch 1988, Wennerberg 2001a, Buehler and Baker 2005) and by the high genetic divergence between shorebird species (Baker and Strauch 1988, L. Wennerberg, unpubl.). The bottlenecks may be related to earlier climatic perturbations (Baker et al. 1994, Wennerberg 2001a). For example, at the beginning of warming periods after ice ages, the Arctic breeding habitat was restricted by the glacial ice covering northern land areas, as well as by vegetation from warmer areas expanding from the south. Together, these two processes minimized the total extent of breeding habitat available for Arctic shorebirds, which may in turn have affected breeding success and eventually population numbers (Kraaijeveld and Nieboer 2000). The consequences are thought to have been most pronounced for the High Arctic specialists such as red knot, for which only small refugial areas are thought to have existed. Accordingly, these are the species that show the lowest genetic variability today (Baker et al. 1994, Wennerberg and Burke 2001, Wennerberg et al. 2002). It remains to be seen whether the reduction in genetic diversity has also reduced their ability to adapt to environmental change, and whether it puts these species more at risk now and in the future.

Acknowledgements

The present review paper is a result of the Pan-Arctic Shorebird Research and Monitoring Workshop held in Denmark 3-6 December 2003. The workshop was organized by Hans Meltofte, Elin Pierce, Aevar Petersen, Liv Wennerberg, and Thomas B. Berg, and it was generously financed by the Nordic Arctic Research Programme under the Nordic Council of Ministers, the Danish Environmental Protection Agency, and the National Environmental Research Institute, Denmark.

The interchange between HM and TP was facilitated by an expeditionary grant from the Netherlands Arctic Programme, administered by the Netherlands Organisation for Scientific Research (NWO). We further thank Craig Ely (USGS) for access to climate and shorebird arrival data from western Alaska, together with Erik Born, Lars Witting and three anonymous referees for suggestions for improvements of the manuscript.

References

Alerstam, T. 1990. Bird migration. – Cambridge University Press, Cambridge.

Alerstam, T., Hjort, C., Högstedt, G., Jönsson, P.E., Karlsson, J. & Larsson, B. 1986. Spring migration of birds across the Greenland inland ice. – Meddelelser om Grønland, Bioscience 21: 38 pp.

Andreev, A.V. 1999. Energetics and survival of birds in extreme environments. – Ostrich 70: 13–22.

Ashkenazie, S. & Safriel, U.N. 1979. Time-Energy Budget of the Semipalmated Sandpiper *Calidris pusilla* at Barrow, Alaska. – Ecology 60: 783-799.

Atkinson, P.W., Clark, N.A., Bell, M.C., Dare, P.J., Clark, J.A. & Ireland, P.L. 2003. Changes in commercially fished shellfish stocks and shorebird populations in the Wash, England. – Biological Conservation 114: 127-141.

Austin, G.E., Peachel, I. & Rehfish, M.M. 2000. Regional trends in coastal wintering waders in Britain. – Bird Study 47: 352-371.

Avise, J.C. 2000. Phylogeography. The history and formation of species. – Harvard University Press, Cambridge, Mass.

Baker, A.J. 1992. Molecular genetics of *Calidris*, with special reference to Knots. – Wader Study Group Bulletin 84, Supplement: 29–35.

Baker, A.J. & Strauch, J.G. 1988. Genetic variation and differentiation in shorebirds. – Acta XX Congressus Internationalis Ornithologicus 2: 1639–1645.

Baker, A.J., Piersma, T. & Rosenmeier, L. 1994. Unraveling the intraspecific phylogeography of Knots *Calidris canutus*: progress report on the search for genetic markers. – Journal für Ornithologie 135: 599-608.

Baker, A.J., González, P.M., Piersma, T., Niles, L.J., de Lima Serrano do Nascimento, I., Atkinson, P.W., Clark, N.A., Minton, C.D.T., Peck, M.K. & Aarts, G. 2004. Rapid population decline in Red Knots: fitness consequences of decreased refuelling rates and late arrival in Delaware Bay. – Proceedings of the Royal Society, London B 271: 875-882.

Barraclough, R.K. (ed.) 2006. Current topics in avian disease research: understanding endemic and invasive diseases. – Ornithological Monographs 60: 1-111.

Bart, J., Brown, S., Harrington, B.A. & Morrison, R.I.G. 2007. Survey trends of North American shorebirds: population declines or shifting distributions? – Journal of Avian Biology 38: 73-82.

Bay, C. 1998. Vegetation mapping of Zackenberg valley, Northeast Greenland. – Danish Polar Center & Botanical Museum, University of Copenhagen. 29 p. Also on ftp://www.dpc.dk/zero/ZACveg.pdf

Bliss, L.C. 1997. Arctic ecosystems of North America. – In: Wielgolaski, F.E. (ed.). Polar and Alpine Tundra. Vol. 3. Elsevier, Amsterdam: 551-683.

Blomqvist, S., Holmgren, N., Åkesson, S., Hedenström, A. & Pettersson, J. 2002. Indirect effects of lemming cycles on sandpiper dynamics: 50 years of counts from southern Sweden. – Oecologia 133: 146-158.

Boertmann, D. 1994. An annotated checklist to the birds of Greenland. – Meddelelser om Grønland, Bioscience 38: 63 pp.

Boyd, H. 1962. Mortality and fertility of the European Charadrii. – Ibis 104: 68-87.

Boyd, H. 1992. Arctic summer conditions and British Knot numbers: An exploratory analysis. – In: Piersma, T. & Davidson, N. (eds). The Migration of Knots. Wader Study Group Bulletin 64, Supplement: 144-152.

Boyd, H. & Madsen, J. 1997. Impacts of Global Change on Arctic-Breeding Bird Populations and Migration. – In: Oechel, W.C., Callaghan, T.V., Gilmanov, T., Holten, J.I., Maxwell, B., Molau, U. & Sveinbjornsson, B. (eds). Global change and Arctic terrestrial ecosystems. Springer Verlag, New York: 201-217.

Boyd, H. & Petersen, A. 2006. Spring arrivals of migrant waders in Iceland. – Ringing & Migration 23: 107-115.

Boyd, H. & Piersma, T. 2001. Changing balance between survival and recruitment explains population trends in red knots *Calidris canutus islandica* wintering in Britain, 1969-1995. – Ardea 89: 301-317.

Brown, S., Bart, J., Lanctot, R.B., Johnson, J.A., Kendall, S., Payer, D. & Johnson, J. 2007. Shorebird abundance and distribution on the coastal plain of the Arctic National Wildlife Refuge. – Condor 109: 1-14.

Bruinzeel, L.W., Piersma, T. & Kersten, M. 1999. Low costs of terrestrial locomotion in waders. – Ardea 87: 199-205.

Buehler, D.M. & A.J. Baker. 2005. Population divergence times and historical demography in Red Knots and Dunlins. – Condor 107: 497-513.

Byrkjedal, I. 1971. Altitude differences in breeding schedules of golden plovers *Pluvialis apricaria* (L.) in South Norway. – Sterna 17: 1-20.

Byrkjedal, I. 1980. Nest predation in relation to snow-cover – a possible factor influencing the start of breeding in shorebirds. – Ornis Scandinavica 11: 249-252.

Byrkjedal, I. 1985. Time-activity budget for breeding Greater Golden-Plovers in Norwegian mountains. – Wilson Bulletin 97: 486-501.

Byrkjedal, I. & Thompson, D.B.A. 1998. Tundra plovers: The Eurasian, Pacific and American golden plovers and grey plover. – T & AD Poyser, London.

Callaghan, T.V., Björn, L.O., Chrnov, Y., Chapin, T., Christensen, T.R., Huntley, B., Ims, R.A., Johansson, M., Jolly, D., Jonasson, S., Matveyeva, N., Panikov, N., Oechel, W. & Shaver, G. 2004. Past Changes in Arctic Terrestrial Ecosystems, Climate and UV Radiation. – Ambio 33: 398-403.

Callaghan, T., Björn, L.O., Chapin III, F.S., Chernov, Y., Christensen, T.R., Huntley, B., Ims, R., Johansson, M., Riedlinger, D.J., Jonasson, S., Matveyeva, N., Oechel, W., Panikov, N., Shaver, G. 2005. Arctic Tundra and Polar Desert Ecosystems. Arctic Climate Impact Assessment, chapter 8. – Cambridge University Press, Cambridge: 243-352.

Cartar, R.V. & Montgomerie, R.D. 1987. Day-to-day variation in nest attentiveness of White-rumped Sandpipers. – Condor 89: 252-260.

Cartar, R.V. & Morrison, R.I.G. 2005. Metabolic correlates of leg length in breeding arctic shorebirds: the cost of getting high. – Journal of Biogeography 32: 377-382.

CAVM Team 2003. Circumpolar Arctic vegetation map. Scale 1:7,500,000. Conservation of Arctic Flora and Fauna (CAFF) Map No. 1. – U.S. Fish and Wildlife Service, Anchorage, Alaska.

CHASM (The Committee for Holarctic Shorebird Monitoring) 2004. Monitoring Arctic-nesting shorebirds: An international vision for the future. – Wader Study Group Bulletin 103: 2-5.

Chernov, Y.I. 1985. The living tundra. – Cambridge Univ. Press, Cambridge.

Comiso, J. C. 2003. Warming Trends in the Arctic from Clear Sky Satellite Observations. – Journal of Climate 16: 3498-3510.

Cramer, W. 1997. Modeling the possible impact of climate change on broad-scale vegetation structure: examples from northern Europe. – In: Oechel, W.C., Callaghan, T.V., Gilmanov, T., Holten, J.I., Maxwell, B., Molau, U. & Sveinbjornsson, B. (eds). Global Change and Arctic Terrestrial Ecosystems. Springer Verlag, New York: 312-329.

Cramp, S. & Simmons, K.E.L. (eds) 1983. The birds of the Western Palearctic. Vol. 3: Waders to gulls. – Oxford University Press.

Davidson, N.C. & Morrison, R.I.G. 1992. Time budgets of prebreeding Knots on Ellesmere Island, Canada. – Wader Study Group Bulletin 64 (Suppl.): 137-143.

Drent, R.H. & Daan, S. 1980. The prudent parent: energetic adjustments in avian breeding. – Ardea 68: 225–252.

Drent, R., Both, C., Green, M., Madsen, J. & Piersma, T. 2003. Pay-offs and penalties of competing migratory schedules. – Oikos 103: 274–292.

Dye, D.G. 2002. Variability and trends in the annual snow-cover cycle in Northern Hemisphere land areas, 1972-2000. – Hydrological Processes 16: 3065-3077.

Dye, D.G. & Tucker, C.J. 2003. Seasonality and trends of snow-cover, vegetation index, and temperature in northern Eurasia. – Geophysical Research Letters 30: 58,1-58,4.

Erckmann, W.J., Jr. 1981. The evolution of sex role reversal and monogamy in shorebirds. – Ph.D. thesis, University of Washington, Seattle.

Evans, P.R. 1991. Seasonal and annual patterns of mortality in migratory shorebirds: some conservation implications. – In: Perrins, C.M., Lebreton, J.-D. & Hirons, G.J.M. (eds). Bird population studies. Relevance to conservation and management. Oxford University Press, Oxford: 346-359

Evans, P.R. 1997. Migratory birds and climate change. – In: Huntley, B., Cramer, C., Morgan, A.V., Prentice, H.C. & Allen, J.R.M. (eds). Past and Future Rapid Environmental Changes: The Spatial and Evolutionary Responses of Terrestrial Biota. Springer, Berlin: 227-238.

Evans, P.R. & Pienkowski, M.W. 1984. Population dynamics of shorebirds. – In: Burger, J. & Olla, B.L. (eds). Behavior of marine animals: V. Shorebirds. Breeding behavior and populations. Plenum Press, New York: 83-123.

Foster, J.L. 1989. The significance of the date of snow disapperance on the arctic tundra as a possible indicator of climate change. – Arctic and Alpine Research 21: 60-70.

Freed, L.A., Cann, R.L., Goff, M.L., Kuntz, W.A. & Bodner, G.R. 2005. Increase in avian malaria at upper elevation in Hawai'i. – Condor 107: 753-764.

Galbraith, H., Jones, R., Park, R., Clohgh, J., Herrod-Julius, S., Harrington, B. & Page, G. 2002. Global climate change and sea level rise: potential losses of intertidal habitat for shorebirds. – Waterbirds 25: 173-183.

Ganter, B. & Boyd, H. 2000. A tropical volcano, high predation pressure, and the breeding biology of Arctic waterbirds: a circumpolar review of breeding failure in the summer of 1992. – Arctic 53: 289-305.

Gill, R.E., Jr. & Handel, C.M. 1990. The importance of subarctic intertidal habitats to shorebirds: a study of the central Yukon-Kuskokwim Delta. – Condor 92: 709-725.

Gill, R.E., Jr., Piersma, T., Hufford, G., Servranckx, R. & Riegen, A. 2005. Crossing the ultimate ecological barrier: evidence for an 11 000-km-long flight from Alaska to New Zealand and eastern Australia by Bar-tailed Godwits. – Condor 107: 1-20.

Goede, A.A. 1993. Longevity in homeotherms, the high lifespan and lifespan energy potential in Charadriiformes. – Ardea 81: 81–88.

Goetz, S.J., Bunn, A.G., Friske, G.J. & Houghton, R.A. 2005. Satellite-observed photosynthetic trends across boreal North America associated with climate and fire disturbance. – Proceedings of the National Academy of Science 102: 13521-13525.

Golovnyuk, V.V., Soloviev, M.Y. & Sviridova, T.V. 2000. Bird fauna in the lower reaches of the Khatanga River, Taimyr Peninsula. – In: Ebbinge, B.S., Mazourov, Yu.L. & Tomkovich, P.S. (eds). Heritage of the Russian Arctic: Research, conservation and international co-operation. Proceedings of the international scientific Willem Barents memorial Arctic conservation symposium (held in Moscow, Russia, 10-14 March 1998). "Ecopros" Publishers, Moscow: 263-270.

REFERENCES

Golovnyuk, V.V., Soloviev, M.Y., Sviridova, T.V., Rakhimberdiyev, E.N. 2004a. Wader number dynamics at southeast of Taimyr Peninsula in 1994-2003. – In: Ryabitsev, V.K. & Korshikov, L.V. (eds). Waders of Eastern Europe and Northern Asia: studies and conservation. Proceedings of the sixth meeting on studies and conservation of waders: 4-7 February 2004, Ekaterinburg: 65-72. In Russian.

Golovnyuk, V.V., Soloviev, M.Y. & Rakhimberdiev, E.N. 2004b. Interesting breeding records of birds on southeast of Taimyr, north-central Siberia. – Ornithologia (Moscow) 31: 214-216.

Gosler, A.G., Greenwood, J.J.D. & Perrins, C. 1995. Predation risk and the cost of being fat. – Nature 377: 621.

Gould, J. 1988. A comparison of avian and mammalian faunas at Lake Hazen, Northwest Territories, in 1961-62 and 1981-82. – Canadian Field-Naturalist 102: 666-670.

Graham, K. 2004. Semipalmated plover breeding success and adult survival: effects of weather and body condition. – M.Sc. thesis. Trent University, Peterborough, ON, Canada.

Gratto-Trevor, C.L. 1991. Parental care in Semipalmated Sandpipers *Calidris pusilla*: brood desertion by females. – Ibis 133: 394-399.

Gratto-Trevor, C.L. 1992. Semipalmated Sandpiper (Calidris pusilla). – In: Poole, A., Stettenheim, P. & Gill, F. (eds). The Birds of North America, No. 6. The Academy of Natural Sciences, Philadelphia, and The American Ornithologists' Union, Washington, D.C.

Gratto-Trevor, C. 1994. Monitoring shorebird populations in the Arctic. – Bird Trends 3: 10-12.

Gratto-Trevor, C.L. 1997. Climate change: Effects on shorebird habitat, prey, and numbers in the outer Mackenzie Delta. – In: Cohen, S. (ed). Mackenzie Basin impact study final report. Environmental Adaptation Research Group, Climate and Atmospheric Research Directorate, Atmospheric Environment Service: 205-210.

Gratto, C.L. & Cooke, F. 1987. Geographic variation in the breeding biology of the Semipalmated Sandpiper. – Ornis Scandinavica 18: 233-235.

Gratto, C.L., Morrison, R.I.G. & Cooke, F. 1985. Philopatry, site tenacity, and mate fidelity in the Semipalmated Sandpiper. – Auk 102: 16-24.

Gratto-Trevor, C.L., Johnston, V.H. & Pepper, S.T. 1998. Changes in shorebird and eider abundance in the Rasmussen Lowlands, NWT. – Wilson Bulletin 110: 316-325.

Gratto-Trevor, C.L., Johnston, V.H. & Pepper, S.T. 2001. Evidence for declines in Arctic populations of shorebirds. – Bird Trends 8: 27-29.

Green, G.H., Greenwood, J.J.D. & Lloyd, C.S. 1977. The influence of snow conditions on the date of breeding of wading birds in north-east Greenland. – Journal of the Zoological Society, London 183: 311-328.

Groisman, P.Y., Karl, T.R. & Knight, R.W. 1994. Changes in Snow Cover, Temperature, and Radiative Heat Balance over the Northern Hemisphere. – Journal of Climate 7: 1633-1656.

Hale, W.G. 1980. Waders. – Collins, London.

Handel, C.M. & Gill, R.E. 2001. Black Turnstone (*Arenaria melanocephala*). – In: Poole, A. & Gill, F. (eds). The Birds of North America, No. 585. The Academy of Natural Sciences, Philadelphia, and The American Ornithologists' Union, Washington, D.C.

Hansen, J. & Meltofte, H. 2006. Birds. In: Klitgaard, A.B., Rasch, M. & Caning, K. (eds.). Zackenberg Ecological Research Operations, 11th Annual Report, 2005. – Danish Polar Center, Ministry of Science, Technology and Innovation, Copenhagen: 43-51.

Henningsson, S.S. & Alerstam, T. 2005. Patterns and determinants of shorebird species richness in the circumpolar Arctic. – Journal of Biogeography 32: 383-396.

Hildén, O. 1965. Zur Brutbiologie des Temminckstrandläufers *Calidris temminckii* (Leisl.). – Ornis Fennica 42: 1-5.

Hildén, O. 1979. Nesting of Temminck's Stint *Calidris temminckii* during an arctic snowstorm. – Ornis Fennica 56: 30-32.

Hillebrand, H. 2004. On the generality of the latitudinal diversity gradient. – American Naturalist 163: 192–211.

Hitchcock, C.L. & Gratto-Trevor, C. 1997. Diagnosing a shorebird local population decline with a stage-structured population model. – Ecology 78: 522-534.

Hodkinson, I.D. 2003. Metabolic cold adaptation in arthropods: a smaller-scale perspective. – Functional Ecology 17: 562-567.

Holmes, R.T. 1966. Breeding ecology and annual cycle adaptations of the red-backed sandpiper (*Calidris alpina*) in northern Alaska. – Condor 68: 3-46.

Holmes, R.T. 1970. Differences in population density, territoriality, and food supply of dunlin on arctic and subarctic tundra. – Symposium of the British Ecological Society 10: 303-319.

Holmes, R.T. 1971a. Latitudinal differences in the breeding and molt schedules of Alaskan Red-backed Sandpipers (*Calidris alpina*). – Condor 73: 93-99.

Holmes, R.T. 1971b. Density, habitat, and the mating system of the Western Sandpiper (*Calidris mauri*). – Oecologia 7: 191-208.

Holmes, R.T. 1972. Ecological factors influencing the breeding season schedule of western sandpipers (*Calidris mauri*) in subarctic Alaska. – American Midland Naturalist 87: 472-491.

Holmes, R.T. & Pitelka, F.A. 1968. Food overlap among coexisting sandpipers on northern Alaskan tundra. – Systematic Zoology 17: 305-318.

Holmgren, M.A., Jönsson, P.E. & Wennerberg, L. 2001. Geographical variation in the timing of breeding and moult in dunlin *Calidris alpina* on the Palearctic tundra. – Polar Biology 24: 369-377.

Houston, A.I. & McNamara, J.M. 1993. A theoretical investigation of the fat reserves and mortality levels of small birds in winter. – Ornis Scandinavica 24: 205-219.

Huntley, B. 1997. The response of vegetation to past and future climate changes. – In: Oechel, W.C., Callaghan, T.V., Gilmanov, T., Holten, J.I., Maxwell, B., Molau, U. & Sveinbjornsson, B. (eds). Global change and Arctic terrestrial ecosystems. Springer Verlag, New York: 290-311.

Hurd, P.D. & Pitelka, F.A. 1954. The role of insects in the economy of certain Arctic Alaskan birds. – Proceedings 3rd Alaskan scientific conference: 136-137.

Högstedt, G. 1974. Lengths of pre-laying period in the Lapwing *Vanellus vanellus* in relation to its food resources. – Ornis Scandinavica 5: 1-4.

Hötker, H. 1995. Avifaunistical Records of the WWF Expeditions to Taimyr in the Years 1989, 1990 and 1991. Faunistik und Naturschutz auf Taimyr. – Corax 16, Sonderheft: 34-89.

International Wader Study Group 2004. Waders are declining worldwide. Conclusions from the 2003 International Wader Study Group Conference, Cádiz, Spain. – Wader Study Group Bulletin 103: 8-12.

Jehl, J. 1979. The autumnal migration of Baird's Sandpipers. – Studies in Avian Biology 2: 55-68.

Jehl, J.R. Jr. & Lin, W. 2001. Population status of shorebirds nesting at Churchill, Manitoba. – Canadian Field-Naturalist 115: 487-494.

Johnston, V.H., Gratto-Trevor, C.L. & Pepper, S.T. 2000. Assessment of bird populations in the Rasmussen Lowlands, Nunavut. – Canadian Wildlife Service Occasional Paper No. 101, 56 pp. Canadian Wildlife Service, Ottawa.

Jonasson, S., Callaghan, T.V., Shaver, G.R. & Nielsen, L.A. 2000. Arctic Terrestrial Ecosystems and Ecosystem Function. – In: Nuttall, M. & Callaghan, T.V. (eds). The Arctic, environment, people, policy. Harwood Academic Publishers: 275-313.

Järvinen, O. & Väisänen, R.A. 1978. Ecological zoogeography of North European waders, or Why do so many waders breed in the North? – Oikos 30: 496-507.

Kania, W. 1990. The primary moult of breeding dunlins Calidris alpina in the central Taymyr in 1989. – Wader Study Group Bulletin 60: 17-19.

Kaplan, J.O. 2005. Climate Change and Arctic Vegetation. – In: Rosentrater, L. (ed) 2° is too much! Evidence and implications of dangerous climate change in the Arctic. WWF International Arctic Programme: 25-41.

Kattsov, V.M., Källén, E., Cattle, H., Christensen, J., Drange, H., Hanssen-Bauer, I., Jóhannesen, T., Karol, I., Räisänen, J., Svensson, G., Vavulin, S., Chen, D., Polyakov, I. & Rinke, A. 2005. Future Climate Change: Modeling and Scenarios for the Arctic. – Arctic Climate Impact Assessment, chapter 4, Cambridge University Press, Cambridge: 99-150.

Klaassen, M., Lindström, Å., Meltofte, H. & Piersma, T. 2001. Arctic waders are not capital breeders. – Nature 413: 794.

Kondratyev, A.Ya. 1982. Biology of waders in tundras of North-East Asia. – Moscow: Nauka Publ. In Russian.

Kraaijeveld, K. & Nieboer, E.N. 2000. Late quaternary paleogeography and evolution of arctic breeding waders. – Ardea 88: 193-205.

Krebs, C.J., Kenney, A.J., Gilbert, S., Danell, K., Angergjörn, A., Erlinge, S., Bromley, R.G., Shank, C. & Carriere, S. 2002. Synchrony in lemming and vole populations in the Canadian Arctic. – Canadian Journal of Zoology 80: 1323-1333.

Krijgsveld, K.L., Reneerkens, J.W.H., McNett, G.D. & Ricklefs, R.E. 2003. Time budgets and body temperatures of American Golden-Plover chicks in relation to ambient temperature. – Condor 105: 268–278.

Lank, D.B., Oring, L.W. & Maxson, S.J. 1985. Mate and nutrient limitation of egg-laying in a polyandrous shorebird. – Ecology 66: 1513-1524.

Lank, D.B., Butler, R.W., Ireland, J. & Ydenberg, C. 2003. Effects of predation danger on migration strategies of sandpipers. – Oikos 103: 303-319.

Lappo, L.G. 1996. Comparisons of breeding range structure for Dunlin *Calidris alpina* and Curlew Sandpiper *Calidris ferruginea:* conservative and nomadic tundra waders. – Wader Study Group Bulletin 80: 41-46.

Lappo, L.G. 2000. Dynamics of bird breeding ranges in the Russian Arctic and Subarctic, with special reference to the Taimyr peninsula. – In: Mazurov, Yu.I., Ebbinge, S. & Tomkovich, P.S. (eds). Heritage of the Russian Arctic: research, conservation and international co-operation. Moscow, Ecopros Publishers: 283-293.

Lappo, L.G. & Tomkovich, P.S. 2006. Limits and structure of the breeding range of the Curlew Sandpiper *Calidris ferruginea*. – In: Underhill, L.G., Tomkovich, P.S. & Harrison, J.A. (eds). The Annual Cycle of the Curlew Sandpiper *Calidris ferruginea*. International Wader Studies 19: 9-18.

Lima, S.L. 1986. Predation risk and unpredictable feeding conditions - determinants of body-mass in birds. – Ecology 67: 377-385.

Lindström, Å. 1998. Mass and Morphometrics of Little Stints on Autumn Migration along the Arctic Coast of Eurasia. – Ibis 140: 171-174.

Lindström, Å. & Agrell, J. 1999. Global change and possible effects on the migration and reproduction of arctic-breeding waders. – Ecological Bulletin 47: 145-159.

Lindström, Å. & Klaassen, M. 2003. High metabolic rates of shorebirds while in the Arctic: a circumpolar view. – Condor 105: 420-427.

Lindström, Å., Klaassen, M., Piersma, T., Holmgren, N. & Wennerberg, L. 2002. Fuel stores of juvenile waders on autumn migration in high arctic Canada. – Ardea 90: 93-101.

Lyngs, P. 2003. Migration and winter ranges of birds in Greenland. – Dansk Ornitologisk Forenings Tidsskrift 97: 1-167.

MacArthur, R. H. 1972. Geographical ecology. – Princeton University Press, Princeton, N.J.

MacLean, S.F. & Pitelka, F.A. 1971. Seasonal patterns of abundance of tundra arthropods near Barrow. – Arctic 24: 19-40.

Marthinsen, G., Wennerberg, L. & Lifjeld, J.T. 2007. Phylogeography and subspecies taxonomy of dunlins (*Calidris alpina*) in western Palearctic analyzed by DNA mi-

REFERENCES

crosatellites and AFLP markers. – Biological Journal of the Linnean Society (in press).

Mayfield, H.F. 1978. Undependable breeding conditions in the Red Phalarope. – Auk 95: 590-592.

Mayfield, H.F. 1979. Red Phalaropes breeding on Bathurst Island. – Living Bird 17: 7-39.

McCaffery, B.J. & Ruthrauff, D.R. 2004a. Spatial variation in shorebird nest success: implications for inference. – Wader Study Group Bulletin 103: 67-70.

McCaffery, B.J. & Ruthrauff, D.R. 2004b. How intensive is intensive enough? Limitations of intensive searching for estimating shorebird nest numbers. – Wader Study Group Bulletin 103: 63-66.

McCaffery, B.J., Bart, J. & Ruthrauff, D.R. 2002. Kanaryarmiut Field Station, Yukon Delta National Wildlife Refuge, Alaska, USA. – In: Soloviev, M.Y. & Tomkovich, P.S. (eds). Arctic birds: Newsletter of international breeding conditions survey, No. 4, International Wader Study Group: 17-18.

McCaffery, B.J., Handel, C.M., Gill Jr., R.E. & Ruthrauff, D.R. 2006. The blind men and the elephant: concerns about the use of juvenile proportion data. – Stilt 50: 141-151.

McCarthy, J.J., Canziani, O.F., Leary, N.A., Dokken, D.J. & White, K.S. (eds) 2001. Intergovernmental panel on climate change third assessment report. Climate change 2001: Impacts, adaptations, and vulnerability. – Cambridge University Press, Cambridge.

Meissner, W. 2004. Variability in the size of juvenile Red Knots *Calidris canutus canutus*. – Wader Study Group Bulletin 103: 71-74.

Meltofte, H. 1976. Ornithological Observations in Southern Peary Land, North Greenland, 1973. – Meddelelser om Grønland 205(1): 57 pp.

Meltofte, H. 1979. The population of waders Charadriidae at Danmarks Havn, Northeast Greenland, 1975. – Dansk Ornitologisk Forenings Tidsskrift 73: 69-94.

Meltofte, H. 1985. Populations and breeding schedules of waders, Charadrii, in high arctic Greenland. – Meddelelser om Grønland, Bioscience 16: 43 pp.

Meltofte, H. 1996. Are African wintering waders really forced south by competition from northerly wintering conspecifics? Benefits and constraints of northern versus southern wintering and breeding in waders. – Ardea 84: 31-44.

Meltofte, H. 1998. Birds. – In: Meltofte, H. & Rasch, M. (eds). Zackenberg ecological research operations, 3rd annual report, 1997. Danish Polar Center, Ministry of Research and Information Technology: 27-31. Also on ftp://www.dpc.dk/zero/ZAR1997.pdf

Meltofte, H. 2000. Birds. – In: Caning, K. & Rasch, M. (eds). Zackenberg ecological research operations, 5th annual report, 1999. Danish Polar Center, Ministry of Research and Information Technology: 32-39. Also on ftp://www.dpc.dk/zero/ZAR1999.pdf

Meltofte, H. 2001. Birds. – In: Caning, K. & Rasch, M. (eds). Zackenberg ecological research operations, 6th annual report, 2000. Danish Polar Center, Ministry of Research and Information Technology: 30-39. Also on ftp://www.dpc.dk/zero/ZAR2000.pdf

Meltofte, H. 2003. Birds. – In: Caning, K. & Rasch, M. (eds). Zackenberg ecological research operations, 7th annual report, 2001. Danish Polar Center, Ministry of Science, Technology and Innovation: 30-39. Also on ftp://www.dpc.dk/zero/ZAR2001.pdf

Meltofte, H. 2006. Wader populations at Zackenberg, high-arctic Northeast Greenland, 1996-2005. – Dansk Ornitologisk Forenings Tidsskrift 100: 16-28.

Meltofte, H. & Berg, T.B. 2004. Zackenberg ecological research operations. BioBasis: Conceptual design and sampling procedures of the biological programme of Zackenberg Basic. 7th edition. – National Environmental Research Institute, Department of Arctic Environment. Also on http://www2.dmu.dk/1_Viden/2_Miljoetilstand/3_natur/biobasis/biobasismanual.asp

Meltofte, H. & Lahrmann, D.P. 2006. Time allocation in Greenland high-arctic waders during summer. – Dansk Ornitologisk Forenings Tidsskrift 100: 75-87.

Meltofte, H., Elander, M. & Hjort, C. 1981. Ornithological observations in Northeast Greenland between 74°30' and 76°00' N. lat., 1976. – Meddelelser om Grønland, Bioscience 3: 52 pp.

Meltofte, H., Durinck, J., Jakobsen, B., Nordstrøm, C. & Rigét, F.F. 2006a. Trends in wader populations in the East Atlantic flyway as shown by numbers of autumn migrants in W Denmark, 1964–2003. – Wader Study Group Bulletin 109: 111–119.

Meltofte, H., Høye, T.T., Schmidt, N.M. & Forchhammer, M.C. 2006b. Differences in food abundance cause inter-annual variation in the breeding phenology of High Arctic waders. – Polar Biology 30: 601-606.

Morozov, V.V. 1998. Distribution of breeding waders in the north-east European Russian tundras. – International Wader Studies 10: 186-194.

Morozov, V.V. & Tomkovich, P.S. 1988. Breeding biology of Red-necked Stint (*Calidris ruficollis*) on Eastern Chukotski Peninsula. – In: Flint, V.E. & Tomkovich, P.S. (eds). Archives of the Zoological Museum, Moscow State University, Moscow: Moscow Univ. Publishers 26: 184-206.

Morrison, R.I.G. 1975. Migration and morphometrics of European Knot and Turnstone on Ellesmere Island, Canada. – Bird-Banding 46: 290-301.

Morrison, R.I.G. 1976. Moult of the Purple Sandpiper Calidris maritima in Iceland. – Ibis 118: 237-246.

Morrison, R.I.G. 1984. Migration systems of some New World shorebirds. – In: Burger, J. & Olla, B.L. (eds). Shorebirds: migration and foraging behavior. Plenum Press, New York: 125-202.

Morrison, R.I.G. 1992. Avifauna of the Ellesmere Island National Park Reserve. – Canadian Wildlife Service Technical Report Series 158. Canadian Wildlife Service, Ottawa. 110 pp.

Morrison, R.I.G. 1997. The use of remote sensing to evaluate shorebird habitats and populations on Prince Charles Island, Foxe Basin, Canada. – Arctic 50: 55-75.

Morrison, R.I.G. 2001. Shorebird population trends and issues in Canada - an overview. – Bird Trends 8: 1-5.

Morrison, R.I.G. 2004. Using Migration Counts from Eastern Canada to Access Productivity of Arctic-breeding Shorebirds in Relation to Climate. – Arctic Climate Impact Assessment (ACIA), AMAP Report 2004: 4, Extended Abstracts, Poster Session A2: Paper 11 (2 pp.).

Morrison, R.I.G. 2006. Body transformations, condition, and survival in Red Knots *Calidris canutus* travelling to breed at Alert, Ellesmere Island, Canada. – Ardea 94: 607–618.

Morrison, R.I.G. & Davidson, N.C. 1990. Migration, body condition and behaviour of shorebirds during spring migration at Alert, Ellesmere Island, N.W.T. – In: Harington, C.R. (ed). Canada's missing dimension. Science and history in the Canadian Arctic Islands. Vol. II. Canadian Museum of Nature, Ottawa.

Morrison, R.I.G. & Hobson, K.A. 2004. Use of body stores in shorebirds after arrival on High Arctic breeding grounds. – Auk 121: 333-344.

Morrison, R.I.G., Aubry, Y., Butler, R.W., Beyersbergen, G.W., Downes, C., Donaldson, G.M., Gratto-Trevor, C.L., Hicklin, P.W., Johnston, V.H. & Ross, R.K. 2001. Declines in North American shorebird populations. – Wader Study Group Bulletin 94: 34-38.

Morrison, R.I.G., Ross, R.K. & Niles, L.J. 2004. Declines in wintering populations of Red Knots in southern South America. – Condor 106: 60-70.

Morrison, R.I.G., Davidson, N.C. & Piersma, T. 2005. Transformations at high latitudes: why do Red Knots bring body stores to the breeding grounds? – Condor 107: 449-457.

Morrison, R.I.G., McCaffery, B.J., Gill, R.E., Skagen, S.K., Jones, S.L., Page, G.W., Gratto-Trevor, C.L. & Andres, B.A. 2006. Population estimates of North American shorebirds, 2006. – Wader Study Group Bulletin 111: 67-85.

Morrison, R.I.G., Davidson, N.C. & Wilson, J.R. 2007. Survival of the fattest: body stores on migration and survival in red knots *Calidris canutus islandica*. – Journal of Avian Biology: 38: 479-487.

Mouritsen, K.N. & Poulin, R. 2002. Parasitism, climate oscillations and the structure of natural communities. – Oikos 97: 462-468.

Myers, J.P. & Pitelka, F.A. 1979. Variations in summer temperature patterns near Barrow, Alaska: analysis and ecological interpretation. – Arctic and Alpine Research 11: 131-144.

Myneni, R.B., Keeling, C.D., Tucker, C.J., Asrar, G. & Nemani, R.R. 1997. Increased plant growth in the northern high latitudes from 1981 to 1991. – Nature 386: 698-702.

Nebel, S. & McCaffery, B.J. 2003. Vocalization activity of breeding shorebirds: documentation of its seasonal decline and applications for breeding bird surveys. – Canadian Journal of Zoology 81: 1702-1708.

Nebel, S., Piersma, T., van Gils, J., Dekinga, A. & Spaans, B. 2000. Length of stopover, fuel storage and a sex-bias in the occurrence of Red Knots *Calidris c. canutus* and *C. c. islandica* in the Wadden Sea during southward migration. – Ardea 88: 165-176.

Nettleship, D.N. 1973. Breeding ecology of Turnstones *Arenaria interpres* at Hazen Camp, Ellesmere Island, NWT. – Ibis 115: 202-217.

Nettleship, D.N. 1974. The breeding of the Knot *Calidris canutus* at Hazen Camp, Ellesmere Island, NWT. – Polarforschung 44: 8-26.

Neville, J.A. 2002. Division of parental roles in the monogamous western sandpiper, Calidris mauri. – M.S. thesis. Univesity of Alaska Fairbanks.

Nol, E., Blanken, M.S. & Flynn, L. 1997. Sources of variation in clutch size, egg size and clutch completion dates of Semipalmated Plovers in Churchill, Manitoba. – Condor 99: 389-396.

Norderhaug, M. 1989. Svalbards fugler. – Dryers Forlag, Oslo.

Norton, D.W. 1972. Incubation schedules of four species of calidridine sandpipers at Barrow, Alaska. – Condor 74: 164-176.

Ottvall, R., Höglund, J., Bensch, S. & Larsson, K. 2004. Population differentiation in the redshank (*Tringa totanus*) as revealed by mitochondrial DNA and amplified fragment polymorphism markers. – In: Ottvall, R. Population ecology and management of waders breeding on coastal meadows. Ph.D. thesis, Lund University, Sweden.

Parmelee, D.F. & Macdonald, S.D. 1960. The birds of west-central Ellesmere Island and adjacent areas. – National Museum of Canada Bulletin 169: 1-303.

Pattie, D.L. 1990. A 16-year record of summer birds on Truelove Lowland, Devon Island, Northwest Territories, Canada. – Arctic 43: 275-283.

Paulson, D. R. 1995. Black-bellied Plover (*Pluvialis squatarola*). – In: Poole, A. & Gill, F. (eds). The Birds of North America, No. 186. The Academy of Natural Sciences, Philadelphia, and The American Ornithologists' Union, Washington, D.C.

Pennycuick, C. J. 1989. Bird flight performance. A practical calculation model. – Oxford University Press, Oxford.

Piersma, T. 1997. Do global patterns of habitat use and migration strategies co-evolve with relative investments in immunocompetence due to spatial variation in parasite pressure? – Oikos 80: 623–631.

Piersma, T. 1998. Phenotypic flexibility during migration: optimization of organ size contingent on the risks and rewards of fueling and flight? – Journal of Avian Biology 29: 511-520.

Piersma, T. 2002. Energetic bottlenecks and other design constraints in avian annual cycles. – Integrative and Comparative Biology 42: 51–67.

Piersma, T. 2003. "Coastal" versus "inland" shorebird species: interlinked fundamental dichotomies between their life- and demographic histories? – Wader Study Group Bulletin 100: 5–9.

Piersma, T. & Lindström, Å. 2004. Migrating shorebirds as in-

REFERENCES

tegrative sentinels of global environmental change. – Ibis 146 (Suppl.1): 61–69.

Piersma, T. & Morrison, R.I.G. 1994. Energy expenditure and water turnover of incubating Ruddy Turnstones: high costs under High Arctic climatic conditions. – Auk 111: 366-376.

Piersma, T. & Wiersma, P. 1996. Family Charadriidae (plovers). – In: del Hoyo, J., Elliott, A. & Sargatal, J. (eds). Handbook of the birds of the world. Vol. 3, Hoatzins to auks. – Lynx Editions, Barcelona: 384-442.

Piersma, T., Klaassen, M., Bruggemann, J.H., Blomert, A.-M., Gueye, A., Ntiamoa-Baidu, Y. & van Brederode, N.E. 1990. Seasonal timing of the spring departure of waders from the Banc d'Arguin, Mauritania. – Ardea 78: 123-134.

Piersma, T., van Gils, J. & Wiersma, P. 1996. Family Scolopacidae (sandpipers, snipes and phalaropes). – In: del Hoyo, J., Elliott, A. & Sargatal, J. (eds). Handbook of the birds of the world. Vol. 3, Hoatzins to auks. Lynx Editions, Barcelona: 444-533.

Piersma, T., Gudmundsson, G.A. & Lilliendahl, K. 1999. Rapid changes in the size of different functional organ and muscle groups during refueling in a long-distance migrating shorebird. – Physiological and Biochemical Zoology 72: 405-415.

Piersma, T, Lindström, Å., Drent, R.H., Tulp, I., Jukema, J., Morrison, R.I.G., Reneerkens, J., Schekkerman, H. & Visser, G.H. 2003. High daily energy expenditure of incubating shorebirds on High Arctic tundra: a circumpolar study. – Functional Ecology 17: 356-362.

Piersma, T., Rogers, D.I., González, P.M., Zwarts, L., Niles, L.J., de Lima Serrano do Nascimento, I., Minton, C.D.T. & Baker, A.J. 2005. Fuel storage rates before northward flights in Red Knots worldwide: facing the severest ecological constraint in tropical intertidal environments? – In: Greenberg, R. & Marra, P.P. (eds). Birds of two worlds: the ecology and evolution of migration. John Hopkins University Press, Baltimore: 262-273.

Pitelka, F.A., 1959. Numbers, breeding schedule, and territoriality in Pectoral Sandpipers of northern Alaska. – Condor 61: 233-264.

Pitelka, F., Holmes, R.T. & Maclean, S.F. 1974. Ecology and Evolution of Social Organisation in Arctic Sandpipers. – American Zoologist 14: 185-204.

Pozdnyakov, V.I. 1997. Lena Delta. – In: Tomkovich, P.S. & Zharikov Y.V. (eds). Breeding conditions for waders in the Russian tundras in 1996. Wader Study Group Bulletin 83: 31-32.

Primmer, C.R., Randsepp, T., Chowdhary, B.P., Moller, A.P. & Ellegren, H. 1997. Low frequency of microsatellites in the avian genome. – Genome Research 7: 471-482.

Rehfisch, M.M. & Crick, H.Q.P. 2003. Predicting the impact of climate change on Arctic-breeding waders. – Wader Study Group Bulletin 100: 86-95.

Rehfisch, M.M., Austin, G.E., Freeman, S.N., Armitage, M.J.S. & Burton, N.H.K. 2004. The possible impact of climate change on the future distributions and numbers of waders on Britain's non-estuary coast. – Ibis 146 (Suppl.1): 70-81.

Reid, J.M., Creswell, W., Holt, S., Mellanby, R.J., Whitfield, D.P. & Ruston, G.D. 2002. Nest scrape design and clutch heat loss in Pectoral Sandpipers Calidris melanotos. – Fuctional Ecology 16: 305-312.

Reynolds, J.D. 1987. Mating system and nesting biology of the red-necked phalarope Phalaropus lobatus: what constrains polyandry? – Ibis 129: 225-242.

Rogacheva, H. 1992. The birds of central Siberia. – Husum Drück- und Verlagsgesellschaft, Husum.

Ross, H. 1979. Multiple clutches and shorebird egg and body-weight. – American Naturalist 113: 618-622.

Roudybush, T.E., Grau, C.R., Peterson, M.R., Ainley, D.G., Hirsch, K.V., Gilman, A.P. & Patten, S.M. 1979. Yolk formation in some charadriiform birds. – Condor 81: 293-298.

Ruthrauff, D.R. 2002. Seasonal and age-related trends in the reproductive output of western sandpipers (Calidris mauri) at Kanaryaraq, Alaska. – M.Sc. thesis, Humboldt State University, Arcata, California.

Ruthrauff, D.R. & McCaffery, B.J. 2005. Survival of western sandpiper broods on the Yukon-Kuskokwim Delta, Alaska. – Condor 107: 597-604.

Ryabitsev, V.K. 1993. Territorial relations and dynamics of bird communities in Subarctic. – Ekaterinburg: Nauka Publ. In Russian.

Ryabitsev, V.K. & Alekseeva, N.S. 1998. Nesting density dynamics and site fidelity of waders on the middle and northern Yamal. – International Wader Studies 10: 195-200.

Ryabitsev, V.K., Ryzhanovsky, V.N. & Shutov, S.V. 1976. Influence of predators on breeding effectiveness of birds in Yamal during number depression of rodents. – Ecologia (USSR) 4: 103-104. In Russian.

Sandercock, B.K. 1998. Chronology of nesting events in Western and Semipalmated sandpipers near the Arctic Circle. – Journal of Field Ornithology 69: 235-243.

Sandercock, B.K. 2003. Estimation of survival rates for wader populations: a review of mark-recapture methods. – Wader Study Group Bulletin 100: 163-174.

Sandercock, B.K. & Gratto-Trevor, C.L. 1997. Local survival in Semipalmated Sandpipers Calidris pusilla breeding at La Pérouse Bay, Canada. – Ibis 139: 305-312.

Sandercock, B.K., Lank, D.B. & Cooke, F. 1999. Seasonal declines in the fecundity of Arctic-breeding sandpipers: Different tactics in two species with an invariant clutch size. – Journal of Avian Biology 30: 460-468.

Schamel, D. 2000. Female and male reproductive strategies in the red-necked phalarope, a polyandrous shorebird. – Ph.D. thesis, Simon Fraser University.

Schamel, D. & Tracy, D.M. 1987. Latitudinal trends in breeding Red Phalaropes. – Journal of Field Ornithology 58: 126-134.

Schamel, D., Tracy, D.M., Schamel, J.T. & Schamel, J. 1999. Nesting waterbird studies at Cape Espenberg, Alaska: a comparison of the 1970s and 1990s. Interim Report. – National Park Service and US Fish & Wildlife Service.

Schamel, D., Tracy, D.M., Schamel, J.T., Schamel, J. & Zharikov, Y. 2003. The effect of a late spring on nesting Western Sandpipers at Cape Espenberg, Alaska. – Abstract of paper at Western Sandpiper Workshop. Simon Fraser University, Burnaby, B.C., Canada. January.

Schamel, J. 1999. A comparative study of productivity of Western Sandpipers (*Calidris mauri*) in western Alaska. – Abstract of paper at the Alaska Statewide High School Science Symposium. Fairbanks, Alaska. March.

Schamel, J.T., Tracy, D.M. & Schamel, D. 2002. The effect of a late spring on nesting Dunlins at Cape Espenberg, Alaska. – Abstract of paper at 9th Alaska Bird Conference. Fairbanks, Alaska. March.

Schekkerman, H. & van Roomen, M. 1995. Breeding waders at Pronchishcheva Lake, Northeastern Taimyr, Siberia, in 1991. – WIWO report 55, Zeist, The Netherlands.

Schekkerman, H., van Roomen, M.J.W. & Underhill, L.G. 1998. Growth, behaviour of broods and weather-related variation in breeding productivity of curlew sandpipers *Calidris ferruginea*. – Ardea 86: 153-168.

Schekkerman, H., Tulp, I., Piersma, T. & Visser, G.H. 2003a. Mechanisms promoting higher growth rate in arctic than in temperate shorebirds. – Oecologia 134: 332-342.

Schekkerman, H., Tulp, I. & Ens, B. 2003b. Conservation of long-distance migratory wader populations: reproductive consequences of events occurring in distant staging sites. – Wader Study Group Bulletin 100: 151-156.

Schekkerman, H., Tulp, I., Calf, K.M. & de Leeuw, J.J. 2004. Studies on breeding shorebirds at Medusa Bay, Taimyr, in summer 2002. – Alterra report 922, Wageningen, The Netherlands.

Schneider, D.C. & Harrington, B.A. 1981. Timing of shorebird migration in relation to prey depletion. – Auk 98: 801-811.

Schwilch, R., Piersma, T., Holmgren, N. & Jenni, L. 2002. Do migratory birds need a nap after a long nonstop flight? – Ardea 90: 149-154.

Smith, P.A. 2003. Factors affecting nest site selection and reproductive success of tundra nesting shorebirds. – M.Sc. thesis, University of British Columbia, Vancouver, B.C.

Smith, P.A., Gilchrist, H.G. & Smith, J.N.M. 2007. Effects of nest habitat, food, and parental behavior on shorebird nest success. – Condor 109: 15-31.

Solomon, A.M. 1997. Natural migration rates of trees: Global terrestrial carbon cycle implications. – In: Huntley, B., Cramer, C., Morgan, A.V., Prentice, H.C. & Allen, J.R.M. (eds). Past and future rapid environmental changes: The spatial and evolutionary responses of terrestrial biota. Springer, Berlin: 455-468.

Soloviev, M.Y. & Pronin, T.A. 1998. Biometrics and primary moult of Dunlin *Calidris alpina* from Taimyr, Siberia. – Ostrich 69: 412-413.

Soloviev, M.Y. & Tomkovich, P.S. 1997. Body mass changes in waders (Charadrii) in a High Arctic area at Northern Taimyr, Siberia. – Journal für Ornithologie 138: 271-281.

Soloviev, M.Y., Golovnyuk, V.V., Rakhimberdiev, E.N. & Gatilov, A.A. 2005. Breeding conditions and numbers of birds on Taimyr, 2004. – Report of the Wader Monitoring Project on Taimyr: http://www.wader.ru/pdf/taim04.pdf.

Soloviev, M.Y., Minton, C.D.T. & Tomkovich, P.S. 2006. Breeding performance of tundra waders in response to rodent abundance and weather from Taimyr to Chukotka, Siberia. – In: Boere, G.C., Galbraith, C.A. & Stroud, D.A. (eds). Waterbirds around the world. The Stationery Office, Edinburgh, UK: 131-137.

Spiekman, H. & Groen, N. 1993. Breeding performance of arctic waders in relation to lemming densities, North-east Taimyr, Siberia, 1992. – WIWO report 33, Zeist, The Netherlands.

Stenseth, N.C. & Ims, R.A. 1993. The biology of lemmings. – Linnean Society Symposium Series, Academic Press.

Stow, D.A., Hope, A., Mcguire, D., Verbyla, D., Gamon, J., Huemmrich, F., Houston, S., Racine, C., Sturm, M., Tape, K., Hinzman, L., Yoshikawa, K., Tweedie, C., Noyle, B., Silapaswan, C., Douglas, D., Griffith, B., Jia, G., Epstein, H., Walker, D., Daeschner, S., Petersen, A., Zhou, L. & Myneni, R. 2004. Remote sensing of vegetation and land-cover change in Arctic Tundra Ecosystems. – Remote Sensing of Environment 89: 281-308.

Sturm, M., Racine, C. & Tape, K. 2001. Increasing shrub abundance in the Arctic. – Nature 411: 546-547.

Summers, R.W. & Underhill, L.G. 1987. Factors related to breeding production of Brent Geese Branta b. bernicla and waders (Charadrii) on the Taimyr Peninsula. – Bird Study 34: 161-171.

Summers, R.W., Underhill, L.G. & Syroechkovski, E.E. 1998. The breeding productivity of dark-bellied brent geese and curlew sandpipers in relation to changes in the numbers of arctic foxes and lemmings on the Taimyr Peninsula, Siberia. – Ecography 21: 573-580.

Sutherland, W.J. 1998. Evidence for flexibility and constraint in migration systems. – Journal of Avian Biology 29: 441-446.

Syroechkovski, E.E., Jr. & Lappo, E.G. 1994. Migration phenology of waders (Charadrii) on the Taimyr Peninsula, northern Russia. – Ostrich 65: 181-190.

Thuman, K.A., Widemo, F. & Piertney, S.B. 2002. Characterization of polymorphic microsatellite DNA markers in the ruff (*Philomachus pugnax*). – Molecular Ecology Notes 2: 276-277.

Tomkovich, P.S. 1985. Sketch of the Purple Sandpiper (*Calidris maritima*) biology on Franz-Josef Land. – Ornithologia (Moscow) 20: 3-17. In Russian.

Tomkovich, P.S. 1988. On peculiarity of breeding biology of Temminck's stint (*Calidris temminckii*) in northern limit of its range. – Ornithologia (Moscow) 23: 188-193. In Russian.

Tomkovich, P.S. 1991. Factors of variation in the clutch size and egg weight in spoon-billed sandpiper (*Eurynorhynchus pygmeus*) (Charadriiformes, Scolopaci-

REFERENCES

dae). – Zoology Zhurnal 70: 107-112. In Russian with English summary.

Tomkovich, P.S. 1994. Site fidelity and spatial structure of population in Rock Sandpiper *Calidris ptilocnemis* and Dunlin *Calidris alpina* on Chukotsky Peninsula. – Russian Journal of Ornithology 3: 13-30. In Russian with English summary.

Tomkovich, P.S. 1995. Breeding biology and breeding success of the spoon-billed sandpiper *Eurynorhynchus pygmeus*. – Russian Journal of Ornithology 4: 77-91. In Russian with English summary.

Tomkovich, P.S. 1998. Breeding schedule and primary moult in Dunlins of the Far East. – Wader Study Group Bulletin 85: 29-34.

Tomkovich, P.S. & Fokin S.Y. 1983. On the ecology of the Temminck's stint in north-east Siberia. – Ornithologia (Moscow) 18: 40-56. In Russian.

Tomkovich, P.S. & Morozov, V.V. 1983. Peculiarities of biology of Western Sandpiper on the Chukotski Peninsula. – Bulleten Moskovskogo Obschestva Ispytatelei Prorody, Otdel Biologichesky 88(5): 38-50. In Russian.

Tomkovich, P.S. & Soloviev, M.Y. 1996. Distribution, migrations and biometrics of Knots (*Calidris canutus*) on Taimyr, Siberia. – Ardea 84: 85-98.

Tomkovich, P.S. & Soloviev, M.Y. 2001. Social organization of Sanderlings breeding at northern Taimyr, Siberia. – Ornithologia (Moscow) 29: 125-136.

Tomkovich, P.S. & Soloviev, M.Y. 2006. Curlew sandpiper *Calidris ferruginea* on their breeding grounds: schedule and geographic distribution in the light of their breeding system. – In: Underhill, L.G., Tomkovich, P.S. & Harrison, J.A. (eds). The Annual Cycle of the Curlew Sandpiper *Calidris ferruginea*. International Wader Studies 19: 19-26.

Tomkovich, P.S. & Syroechkovski, E.E., Jr. 2005. Breeding of Semipalmated Plover *Charadrius semipalmatus* in Russia. – Russian Journal of Ornithology 14, Express-issue No. 298: 795-799. In Russian with English summary.

Tomkovich, P.S., Soloviev, M.Y. & Syroechkovski, E.E., Jr. 1994. Birds of Arctic tundras of Northern Taimyr (Knipovich Bay area). – In: Rogacheva, E.V. (ed). Arctic tundras of Taimyr and Kara Sea islands: Nature, fauna and conservation problems. Vol. 1. Moscow: Inst. of Ecol. and Evolution, Russian Acad. Sci.: 44-110. In Russian.

Tomkovich, P.S., Syroechkovski, E.E., Jr., Lappo, E.G. & Zoeckler, C. 2002. First indications of a sharp population decline in the globally threatened Spoon-billed Sandpiper, *Eurynorhynchus pygmeus*. – Bird Conservation International 12: 1-18.

Troy, D.M. 1996. Population dynamics of breeding shorebirds in Arctic Alaska. – In: Hicklin, P., Erskine, A.J. & Jehl, J. (eds). Shorebird ecology and conservation in the Western Hemisphere. – International Wader Studies 8: 15-27.

Tulp, I. & Schekkerman, H. 2001. Studies on breeding shorebirds at Medusa Bay, Taimyr, in summer 2001. – Alterra report 451, Wageningen, The Netherlands.

Tulp, I. & Schekkerman, H. 2006. Time allocation between feeding and incubation in uniparental arctic-breeding shorebirds: energy reserves provide leeway in a tight schedule. – Journal of Avian Biology 37: 207-218.

Tulp, I. & Schekkerman, H. 2007. Correlates of growth rates in arctic shorebird chicks: timing of snow melt, daily weather and food abundance. – In: Tulp, I. The arctic pulse. Timing of breeding in long-distance migrant shorebirds. PhD thesis, University of Groningen.

Tulp, I. & Schekkerman, H. in press. Climate change advances prey availability for arctic birds: hindcasting the abundance of tundra arthropods using weather and seasonal variation. – Arctic.

Tulp, I., Bruinzeel, L. Jukema, J. & Stepanova, O. 1997. Breeding waders at Medusa Bay, western Taimyr, in 1996. – WIWO report 57, Zeist, The Netherlands.

Tulp, I., Schekkerman, H., Piersma, T., Jukema, J., de Goeij, P. & van de Kam, J. 1998. Breeding waders at Cape Sterlegova, Northern Taimyr, in 1994. – WIWO report 61, Zeist, The Netherlands.

Tulp, I., Schekkerman, H. & Klaassen, R. 2000. Studies on breeding shorebirds at Medusa Bay, Taimyr, in summer 2000. – Alterra report 219, Wageningen, The Netherlands.

Tulp, I., Schekkerman, H., Chylarecki, P., Tomkovich, P., Soloviev, M., Bruinzeel, L., van Dijk, K., Hildén, O., Hötker, H., Kania, W., van Roomen, M., Sikora, A., Summers, R. 2002. Body mass patterns of Little Stints during incubation and chick-rearing at different latitudes. – Ibis 144: 122-134.

Tulp, I., Schekkerman, H., Visser, G.H., Bruinzeel, L.W. & Jukema, J. 2007. Incubation and chick-rearing in high arctic breeding shorebirds: what is the most demanding phase? – In: Tulp, I. The arctic pulse. Timing of breeding in long-distance migrant shorebirds. PhD thesis, University of Groningen.

Underhill, L.G., Prys-Jones, R.P., Syroechkowski, E.E., Jr., Groen, N.M., Karpov, V., Lappo, H.G., van Roomen, M.W.J., Rybkin, A., Schekkerman, H., Spiekman, H. & Summers, R.W. 1993. Breeding of waders (Charadrii) and Brent Geese Branta bernicla bernicla at Pronchishcheva Lake, northeastern Taimyr, Russia, in a peak and a decreasing lemming year. – Ibis 135: 277-292.

van de Kam, J., Ens, B.J., Piersma, T. & Zwarts, L. 2004. Shorebirds. An illustrated behavioural ecology. – KNNV Publishers, Utrecht.

van Gils, J.A., Dekinga, A., Spaans, B., Vahl, W.K. & Piersma, T. 2005a. Digestive bottleneck affects foraging decisions in red knots *Calidris canutus*. II. Patch choice and length of working day. – Journal of Animal Ecology 74: 120-130.

van Gils, J.A., Battley, P.F., Piersma, T. & Drent, R. 2005b. Reinterpretation of gizzard sizes of red knots world-wide emphasises overriding importance of prey quality at migratory stopover sites. – Proceedings of the Royal Society, B 272: 2609-2618.

van Treuren, R., Bijlsma, R., Tinbergen, J.M., Heg, D. & van de

Zande, L. 1999. Genetic analysis of the population structure of socially organized oystercatchers *(Haematopus ostralegus)* using microsatellites. – Molecular Ecology 8: 181-187.

Väisänen, R.A. 1977. Geographic variation in timing of breeding and egg size in eight European species of waders. – Annales Zoologica Fennici 14: 1-25.

Walsh, J.E., Anisimov, O., Hagen, J.O.M., Jakobsson, T., Oerlemans, J., Prowse, T.D., Romanovsky, V., Savelieva, N., Serreze, M., Shiklomanov, I. & Solomon, S. 2005. Cryosphere and Hydrology. Arctic Climate Impact Assessment, chapter 8. – Cambridge University Press, Cambridge: 243-352.

Weber, T.P., Ens, B.J. & Houston, A.I. 1998. Optimal avian migration: a dynamic model of fuel stores and site use. – Evolutionary Ecology 12: 377-402.

Wenink, P.W., Baker, A.J. & Tilanus, M.G.J. 1993. Hypervariable control region sequences reveal global population structuring in a long-distance migrant shorebird, the dunlin *(Calidris alpina)*. – Proceedings of the National Academy of Sciences of the United States of America 90: 94-98.

Wenink, P.W., Baker, A.J., Rösner, H.-U. & Tilanus, M.G.J. 1996. Global mitochondrial DNA phylogeography of Holarctic breeding dunlins *(Calidris alpina)*. – Evolution 50: 318-330.

Wennerberg, L. 2001a. Genetic variation and migration of waders. – Ph.D. thesis, Lund University, Sweden.

Wennerberg, L. 2001b. Breeding origin and migration pattern of dunlin *(Calidris alpina)* revealed by mitochondrial DNA analysis. – Molecular Ecology 10: 1111-1120.

Wennerberg, L. & Bensch, S. 2001. Geographical variation in the Dunlin *Calidris alpina* as revealed by morphology, mtDNA and microsatellites. – In: Wennerberg, L. Genetic variation and migration of waders. Ph.D. thesis, Lund University, Sweden.

Wennerberg, L. & Burke, T. 2001. Low genetic differentiation between Curlew Sandpiper *(Calidris ferruginea)* populations with highly divergent migratory directions shown by mitochodrial DNA and microsatellite analysis. – In: Wennerberg, L. Genetic variation and migration of waders. Ph.D. thesis, Lund University, Sweden.

Wennerberg, L., Holmgren, N., Jönsson, P-E, von Schantz, T. 1999. Genetic and morphological variation in Dunlin *Calidris alpina* breeding in the Palearctic tundra. – Ibis 141: 391-398.

Wennerberg, L., Klaassen, M. & Lindström, Å. 2002. Geographical variation and population structure in the White-rumped Sandpiper *Calidris fuscicollis* as shown by morphology, mitochondrial DNA and carbon isotope ratios. – Oecologia 131: 380-390.

Whitfield, D.P. 1995. Behaviour and ecology of a polyandrous population of Grey Phalaropes *Phalaropus fulicarius* in Iceland. – Journal of Avian Biology 26: 349-352.

Whitfield, D.P & Tomkovich, P.S. 1996. Mating system and timing of breeding in Holarctic waders. – Biological Journal of the Linnean Society 57: 277-290.

Wiersma, P. & Piersma, T. 1994. Effects of microhabitat, flocking, climate and migratory goal on energy expenditure in the annual cycle of Red Knots. – Condor 96, 257-279.

Witter, M.S., Cuthill, I.C. & Bonser, R.H. 1994. Experimental investigations of mass-dependent predation risk in the European starling, *Sturnus vulgaris*. – Animal Behaviour 48: 201-222.

Yarbrough, C.G. 1970. Summer lipid levels of some subarctic birds. – Auk 87: 100-110.

Zhou, L., Tucker, C.J., Kaufmann, R.K., Slayback, D., Shabanov, N.V. & Myneni, R.B. 2001. Variations in northern vegetation activity inferred from satellite data of vegetation index during 1981 to 1999. – Journal of Geophysical Research 106: 20069-20083.

Zwarts, L., Blomert, A.-M. & Wanink, J.H. 1992. Annual and seasonal variation in the food supply harvestable by knot *Calidris canutus* staging in the Wadden Sea in late summer. – Marine Ecology, Progress Series 83: 129-139.

Zöckler, C. & Lysenko, I. 2000. Water birds on the edge. First circumpolar assessment of climate change impact on Arctic breeding water birds. – World Conservation Monitoring Centre, Cambridge.

Appendix

Account of study sites

Below, each main study site is presented with geographical coordinates, shorebird species studied, contributing authors, study years and references to site and methodology descriptions.

Yukon-Kuskokwim Delta, Kanaryarmiut Field Station, Low Arctic Alaska, U.S.A., 61°22'N, 165°08'W, bar-tailed godwit *Limosa lapponica*, western sandpiper *Calidris mauri*, pectoral sandpiper *C. melanotos*, rock sandpiper *C. ptilocnemis*, dunlin *C. alpina*, 1998-2004, B.J. McCaffery, D.R. Ruthrauff, and M. Johnson (Ruthrauff 2002, McCaffery and Ruthrauff 2004a, Nebel and McCaffery 2003).

Cape Espenberg, Low Arctic Seward Peninsula, Alaska, USA, 66°30'N, 163°30'W, semipalmated sandpiper *Calidris pusilla*, western sandpiper, dunlin, red phalarope *Phalaropus fulicarius*, red-necked phalarope *Phalaropus lobatus*, 1976-79, 1994-99, and 2001, D. Schamel and D.M. Tracy (Schamel and Tracy 1987).

Churchill, subarctic Manitoba, Canada, 58°45'N, 95°04'W, semipalmated plover *Charadrius semipalmatus*, 1988-2004, E. Nol and K. Graham (Nol *et al.* 1997).

La Pérouse Bay, near Churchill, subarctic Manitoba, Canada, 58°45'N, 93°25'W, semipalmated sandpiper, 1980-1987, C.L. Gratto-Trevor (Gratto *et al.* 1985, Gratto and Cooke 1987, Hitchcock and Gratto-Trevor 1997).

Rowley Island, High Arctic Foxe Basin, Nunavut, Canada, 68°56'N, 79°18'W, ruddy turnstone *Arenaria interpres*, 1980-1985, R.I.G. Morrison (Piersma and Morrison 1994, Morrison 1997).

Alert, High Arctic Ellesmere Island, Nunavut, Canada, 82°30N, 62°20'W, red knot, ruddy turnstone, sanderling *Calidris alba*, 1974-2004, R.I.G. Morrison (Morrison 1975, Morrison and Davidson 1990, Morrison and Hobson 2004).

Zackenberg, High Arctic Northeast Greenland, 74°30'N, 20°30'W, common ringed plover *Charadrius hiaticula*, red knot, sanderling, dunlin and ruddy turnstone, 1995-2004, H. Meltofte (Bay 1998, Meltofte and Berg 2004).

Gamvik, Low Arctic Finnmark, northernmost Norway, 71°05'N, 28°25'E, dunlin, 1991-2004, H.-U. Rösner and B. Ganter (unpubl.).

Medusa Bay, High Arctic south-western Taimyr, Russia, 73°04'N, 80°30'E, little stint *C. minuta*, dunlin, curlew sandpiper *Calidris ferruginea*, pectoral sandpiper, ruff *Philomachus pugnax*, ruddy turnstone, Pacific golden-plover *Pluvialis fulva*, common ringed plover, 2000-2002, I. Tulp and H. Schekkerman (Tulp *et al.* 2000, Tulp and Schekkerman 2001, Schekkerman *et al.* 2004).

Knipovich Bay, High Arctic northern Taimyr, Russia, 76°04'N, 98°32'E, sanderling, red knot, curlew sandpiper and little stint, 1990-1992, P. Tomkovich and M. Soloviev (Tomkovich *et al.* 1994, Tomkovich and Soloviev 1996, 2001, 2006, Soloviev and Tomkovich 1997, and some others).

Lower Khatanga River, sub-/Low Arctic south-eastern Taimyr, Russia, 72°51'N, 106°02'E, dunlin, little stint, pectoral sandpiper, red phalarope, ruff, Pacific golden-plover and black-bellied plover *Pluvialis squatarola*, 1994-2003, M.Y. Soloviev and V.V. Golovnyuk (Golovnyuk *et al.* 2000, M.Y. Soloviev and V.V. Golovnyuk, unpubl.).

Uelen, Low Arctic Chukotsky Peninsula, Chukotka, Russia, 66°10'N, 169°50'W, red-necked stint *Calidris ruficollis*, western, Baird's *C. bairdii*, and rock sandpipers, dunlin, 1978-1980, P. Tomkovich (Tomkovich and Morozov 1983, Morozov and Tomkovich 1988, and several more, all in Russian).

Belyaka Spit, Low Arctic Chukotsky Peninsula, Chukotka, Russia, 67°04'N, 174°35'W, spoon-billed sandpiper *Eurynorhynchus pygmeus*, 1986-1988, 2002, P.S. Tomkovich (Tomkovich 1991, 1995, and several more).